OPPOSING VIEWPOINTS® SERIES

Privacy

Other Books of Related Interest:

Opposing Viewpoints Series

Cybercrime

Hacking and Hackers

Human Rights

Teenage Sexuality

At Issue Series

Are Social Networking Sites Harmful?

Drones

Location-Based Social Networking and Services

Current Controversies Series

Mobile Apps

Modern-Day Piracy

"Congress shall make no law . . . abridging the freedom of speech, or of the press."

First Amendment to the US Constitution

The basic foundation of our democracy is the First Amendment guarantee of freedom of expression. The Opposing Viewpoints series is dedicated to the concept of this basic freedom and the idea that it is more important to practice it than to enshrine it.

Privacy

Noël Merino, Book Editor

GREENHAVEN PRESS
A part of Gale, Cengage Learning

GALE
CENGAGE Learning·

Farmington Hills, Mich • San Francisco • New York • Waterville, Maine
Meriden, Conn • Mason, Ohio • Chicago

GALE
CENGAGE Learning

Patricia Coryell, *Vice President & Publisher, New Products & GVRL*
Douglas Dentino, *Manager, New Products*
Judy Galens, *Acquisitions Editor*

For more information, contact:
Greenhaven Press
27500 Drake Rd.
Farmington Hills, MI 48331-3535
Or you can visit our Internet site at gale.cengage.com

For product information and technology assistance, contact us at

Gale Customer Support, 1-800-877-4253
For permission to use material from this text or product, submit all requests online at www.cengage.com/permissions

Further permissions questions can be emailed to permissionrequest@cengage.com

Articles in Greenhaven Press anthologies are often edited for length to meet page requirements. In addition, original titles of these works are changed to clearly present the main thesis and to explicitly indicate the author's opinion. Every effort is made to ensure that Greenhaven Press accurately reflects the original intent of the authors. Every effort has been made to trace the owners of copyrighted material.

Cover Image copyright © Carlos Amarillo/Shutterstock.com.

LIBRARY OF CONGRESS CATALOGING-IN-PUBLICATION DATA

Privacy / Noël Merino, book editor.
     pages cm -- (Opposing viewpoints)
    Includes bibliographical references and index.
    ISBN 978-0-7377-7282-1 (hardback) -- ISBN 978-0-7377-7283-8 (paperback)
    1. Privacy, Right of--United States--Juvenile literature. I. Merino, Noël, editor.
    KF1262.P739 2014
    323.44'80973--dc23
                                2014030631

Printed in the United States of America
1 2 3 4 5   19 18 17 16 15

Contents

Why Consider Opposing Viewpoints   11

Introduction   14

Chapter 1: Do Technological Developments Threaten Privacy?

Chapter Preface   19

1. Tracking Is an Assault on Liberty,   21
   with Real Dangers
   Nicholas Carr

2. No More Privacy Paranoia   28
   Farhad Manjoo

3. iSPY: How the Internet Buys and Sells   35
   Your Secrets
   Jamie Bartlett

4. Obscurity in Using Technology Is More   43
   Important than Privacy
   Woodrow Hartzog and Evan Selinger

Periodical and Internet Sources Bibliography   50

Chapter 2: Do Security Measures Infringe on Privacy Rights?

Chapter Preface   52

1. NSA Surveillance Threatens Privacy and Security   54
   Bruce Schneier

2. Privacy Concerns About NSA Intelligence   60
   Gathering Are Unfounded
   Gary Schmitt

3. Privacy Is a Red Herring: The Debate Over NSA   65
   Surveillance Is About Something Else Entirely
   Rosa Brooks

4. The Use of Surveillance Drones Is a Threat   **72**
   to Privacy
   Andrew Napolitano

5. Privacy Concerns Should Not Stunt   **76**
   the Growth of the Drone Industry
   Pierre Hines

6. Biometrics Are the Future of Identification   **82**
   Tim De Chant

7. Biometric Identification Raises Privacy   **93**
   Concerns Without Increasing Security
   Katitza Rodriguez

Periodical and Internet Sources Bibliography   **98**

Chapter 3: Is Medical Privacy Adequately Protected?

Chapter Preface   **100**

1. Private DNA Tests Raise a Variety   **102**
   of Privacy Concerns
   Benjamin Winterhalter

2. The FDA Could Set Personal Genetics   **113**
   Rights Back Decades
   Gary Marchant

3. How ObamaCare Destroys Your Privacy   **121**
   Betsy McCaughey

4. The National Electronic Health Care Database   **125**
   Improves Health Care
   Kathleen Sebelius

Periodical and Internet Sources Bibliography   **129**

Chapter 4: How Should Privacy Be Protected?

Chapter Preface   131

1. Privacy in the Age of Surveillance   133
   Dinah PoKempner

2. An Overreach for the NSA's Critics   141
   Charles C.W. Cooke

3. Big Data, Public and Private   148
   Paul Pillar

4. A Consumer Bill of Rights Is Needed   154
   to Protect Privacy on the Internet
   White House

5. Fourth Amendment Protections Need   159
   Revision to Protect Privacy
   David Cole

Periodical and Internet Sources Bibliography   164

For Further Discussion   165

Organizations to Contact   167

Bibliography of Books   171

Index   174

Why Consider Opposing Viewpoints?

> *"The only way in which a human being can make some approach to knowing the whole of a subject is by hearing what can be said about it by persons of every variety of opinion and studying all modes in which it can be looked at by every character of mind. No wise man ever acquired his wisdom in any mode but this."*
>
> *John Stuart Mill*

In our media-intensive culture it is not difficult to find differing opinions. Thousands of newspapers and magazines and dozens of radio and television talk shows resound with differing points of view. The difficulty lies in deciding which opinion to agree with and which "experts" seem the most credible. The more inundated we become with differing opinions and claims, the more essential it is to hone critical reading and thinking skills to evaluate these ideas. Opposing Viewpoints books address this problem directly by presenting stimulating debates that can be used to enhance and teach these skills. The varied opinions contained in each book examine many different aspects of a single issue. While examining these conveniently edited opposing views, readers can develop critical thinking skills such as the ability to compare and contrast authors' credibility, facts, argumentation styles, use of persuasive techniques, and other stylistic tools. In short, the Opposing Viewpoints Series is an ideal way to attain the higher-level thinking and reading skills so essential in a culture of diverse and contradictory opinions.

In addition to providing a tool for critical thinking, Opposing Viewpoints books challenge readers to question their own strongly held opinions and assumptions. Most people form their opinions on the basis of upbringing, peer pressure, and personal, cultural, or professional bias. By reading carefully balanced opposing views, readers must directly confront new ideas as well as the opinions of those with whom they disagree. This is not to argue simplistically that everyone who reads opposing views will—or should—change his or her opinion. Instead, the series enhances readers' understanding of their own views by encouraging confrontation with opposing ideas. Careful examination of others' views can lead to the readers' understanding of the logical inconsistencies in their own opinions, perspective on why they hold an opinion, and the consideration of the possibility that their opinion requires further evaluation.

Evaluating Other Opinions

To ensure that this type of examination occurs, Opposing Viewpoints books present all types of opinions. Prominent spokespeople on different sides of each issue as well as well-known professionals from many disciplines challenge the reader. An additional goal of the series is to provide a forum for other, less known, or even unpopular viewpoints. The opinion of an ordinary person who has had to make the decision to cut off life support from a terminally ill relative, for example, may be just as valuable and provide just as much insight as a medical ethicist's professional opinion. The editors have two additional purposes in including these less known views. One, the editors encourage readers to respect others' opinions—even when not enhanced by professional credibility. It is only by reading or listening to and objectively evaluating others' ideas that one can determine whether they are worthy of consideration. Two, the inclusion of such viewpoints encourages the important critical thinking skill of objectively evaluating an author's credentials and bias. This evaluation will illuminate an author's reasons for taking a particular stance on an issue and will aid in readers' evaluation of the author's ideas.

It is our hope that these books will give readers a deeper understanding of the issues debated and an appreciation of the complexity of even seemingly simple issues when good and honest people disagree. This awareness is particularly important in a democratic society such as ours in which people enter into public debate to determine the common good. Those with whom one disagrees should not be regarded as enemies but rather as people whose views deserve careful examination and may shed light on one's own.

Thomas Jefferson once said that "difference of opinion leads to inquiry, and inquiry to truth." Jefferson, a broadly educated man, argued that "if a nation expects to be ignorant and free . . . it expects what never was and never will be." As individuals and as a nation, it is imperative that we consider the opinions of others and examine them with skill and discernment. The Opposing Viewpoints series is intended to help readers achieve this goal.

David L. Bender and Bruno Leone,
Founders

Introduction

> *"The Constitution does not explicitly mention any right of privacy. In a line of decisions, however, going back perhaps as far as* Union Pacific [Railway] Co. v. Botsford *(1891), the court has recognized that a right of personal privacy, or a guarantee of certain areas or zones of privacy, does exist under the Constitution."*
>
> *—Justice Harry Blackmun, majority opinion,* Roe v. Wade, *January 22, 1973*

The right to privacy, although not explicitly mentioned in the US Constitution, has come to be recognized as a fundamental right of all Americans. The US Supreme Court first explicitly elaborated on the constitutional foundation of the right to privacy in the 1965 case of *Griswold v. Connecticut*, a case challenging a state law that banned the sale of birth control. In *Griswold*, the court determined that states were not legally allowed to ban the sale of contraceptives to married couples and also that there is an implicit right to marital privacy that is constitutionally guaranteed under the Bill of Rights. A few years later, the court determined that the right to privacy regarding contraceptives also extends to unmarried people. The right to privacy was vital to the landmark Supreme Court ruling in *Roe v. Wade* (1973), wherein the court upheld a woman's right to abortion. Since then, the right to privacy has been cited in several contexts beyond reproductive decisions, including privacy in one's home and privacy in one's activities.

The justification of the right to privacy given in *Griswold* by Justice William O. Douglas appeals to several amendments within the Bill of Rights:

> Specific guarantees in the Bill of Rights have penumbras, formed by emanations from those guarantees that help give them life and substance. Various guarantees create zones of privacy. The right of association contained in the penumbra of the First Amendment is one. . . . The Third Amendment, in its prohibition against the quartering of soldiers "in any house" in time of peace without the consent of the owner, is another facet of that privacy. The Fourth Amendment explicitly affirms the "right of the people to be secure in their persons, houses, papers, and effects, against unreasonable searches and seizures." The Fifth Amendment, in its self-incrimination clause, enables the citizen to create a zone of privacy that government may not force him to surrender to his detriment. The Ninth Amendment provides: "the enumeration in the Constitution, of certain rights, shall not be construed to deny or disparage others retained by the people."

Thus, Douglas claims that the right to privacy is implicitly guaranteed based on several explicit rights guaranteed by the US Constitution.

The Fourth Amendment lends much to the privacy debate in the context of law enforcement searches and seizures. In 1967 the Supreme Court in *Katz v. United States* ruled that the Fourth Amendment grants protection from searches and seizures in all areas where a person has a "reasonable expectation of privacy." Justice John Marshall Harlan II summarized the reasoning in a concurring opinion, finding:

> (a) that an enclosed telephone booth is an area where, like a home, and unlike a field, a person has a constitutionally protected reasonable expectation of privacy; (b) that electronic, as well as physical, intrusion into a place that is in this sense private may constitute a violation of the Fourth

Amendment, and (c) that the invasion of a constitutionally protected area by federal authorities is, as the court has long held, presumptively unreasonable in the absence of a search warrant.

This decision recognized that technology can create a need for further elaboration of the Fourth Amendment's protection against searches and seizures in a private zone, and *Katz* widened that zone of privacy to include not only physical searches by law enforcement, but also monitoring of electronic media.

This constitutional right to privacy recognized by the court is only one facet of privacy protection in the United States. Legislation has been passed to protect personal information, for instance. The Federal Trade Commission (FTC) has been given authority to protect personal information held by the federal government through the Privacy Act of 1974. The Gramm-Leach-Bliley Act, also known as the Financial Services Modernization Act of 1999, regulates financial institutions, thereby protecting private financial information of customers, and the Fair Credit Reporting Act regulates consumer-reporting agencies. The Children's Online Privacy Protection Act limits the collection of information from children, giving parents the opportunity to consent to any use of information from children. No such legislation protects adult data collection.

The right to privacy is one of the most cherished and controversial rights in America, but opposing arguments exist about how to define the right, how to balance the right with other interests, and how to determine when the right has been violated. In *Opposing Viewpoints: Privacy*, authors take a variety of opinions on the subject of privacy in chapters titled "Do Technological Developments Threaten Privacy?," "Do Security Measures Infringe on Privacy Rights?," "Is Medical Privacy Adequately Protected?," and "How Should Privacy Be Protected?" The divergent viewpoints in this volume illustrate that there is wide disagreement about the existing threats to privacy and the manner by which privacy should be protected.

OPPOSING
VIEWPOINTS®
SERIES

CHAPTER 1

Do Technological Developments Threaten Privacy?

Chapter Preface

The technological developments of the last few decades have profoundly altered the privacy landscape. The development of mobile phones and the growth of the Internet are the two most drastic changes widely adopted by most people that raise new questions about what privacy entails and how it should be protected. Newer technologies such as biometric identification and radio-frequency identification (RFID) stand to further challenge ideas about privacy.

Widespread use of mobile phones has only existed for about two decades. In that time, the technology has evolved from a device simply for communication to a small computer that can perform functions such as online shopping, e-mailing, and money transfer. Unlike any device carried by people in the past, modern cell phones now leave a trail of geolocation data, such that when a phone is on, a record of every movement its user makes is logged and often stored for many months.

The Internet has profoundly changed the way people receive information, do work, and engage in commerce. An average user will leave a trail of information each week that shows what the person was searching for, reading, and buying. Prior to such technology, an individual could avoid leaving such a trail by reading printed books and magazines and paying cash for all in-person purchases.

Biometric technology is likely to be more extensively used in the future, relying on the physiological characteristics of a person—such as fingerprints, iris recognition, and DNA—to establish identification, rather than the old-fashioned wallet ID with a photo. Biometric information is more personal—some would say more private—than a mere photo. Radio-frequency identification is already used to track objects, livestock, and pets. If RFID starts to be used on personal items of clothing or even within people, a whole realm of privacy questions will be raised about the ensuing data.

As the authors in this chapter illustrate, there is widespread debate about how the data inherent in these new technologies ought to be handled and whether the benefits of these new technologies outweigh the lowered level of privacy inherent in using them.

> *"The greatest danger posed by the continuing erosion of personal privacy is that it may lead us as a society to devalue the concept of privacy, to see it as outdated and unimportant."*

Tracking Is an Assault on Liberty, with Real Dangers

Nicholas Carr

In the following viewpoint, Nicholas Carr argues that the idea of privacy is under attack by the way in which information is given up online. Carr contends that most people are unaware of how much information is collected about them when they are online and how much privacy they are unwittingly relinquishing. Beyond the danger posed to our concept of privacy, Carr claims that a lack of personal privacy online creates the possibility for criminal harm and marketing manipulation. Carr concludes that better safeguards are needed to protect online privacy. Carr is the author of The Shallows: What the Internet Is Doing to Our Brains.

As you read, consider the following questions:

1. According to the author, what competing value is at odds with privacy online?

2. Carr claims that researchers have found that most Americans can be identified by name and address with only what three pieces of information?

3. According to Carr, what could software makers and website operators do to safeguard online privacy?

In a 1963 Supreme Court opinion, Chief Justice Earl Warren observed that "the fantastic advances in the field of electronic communication constitute a great danger to the privacy of the individual." The advances have only accelerated since then, along with the dangers. Today, as companies strive to personalize the services and advertisements they provide over the Internet, the surreptitious collection of personal information is rampant. The very idea of privacy is under threat.

Most of us view personalization and privacy as desirable things, and we understand that enjoying more of one means giving up some of the other. To have goods, services and promotions tailored to our personal circumstances and desires, we need to divulge information about ourselves to corporations, governments or other outsiders.

This trade-off has always been part of our lives as consumers and citizens. But now, thanks to the Net, we're losing our ability to understand and control those trade-offs—to choose, consciously and with awareness of the consequences, what information about ourselves we disclose and what we don't. Incredibly detailed data about our lives are being harvested from online databases without our awareness, much less our approval.

Even though the Internet is a very social place, we tend to access it in seclusion. We often assume that we're anonymous as we go about our business online. As a result, we treat the Net not just as a shopping mall and a library but as a personal diary and, sometimes, a confessional. Through the sites we visit and the searches we make, we disclose details not only about our jobs, hobbies, families, politics and health, but also about our secrets, fantasies, even our peccadilloes.

But our sense of anonymity is largely an illusion. Pretty much everything we do online, down to individual keystrokes and clicks, is recorded, stored in cookies and corporate databases, and connected to our identities, either explicitly through our user names, credit card numbers and the IP addresses assigned to our computers, or implicitly through our searching, surfing and purchasing histories.

A few years ago, the computer consultant Tom Owad published the results of an experiment that provided a chilling lesson in just how easy it is to extract sensitive personal data from the Net. Mr. Owad wrote a simple piece of software that allowed him to download public wish lists that Amazon.com customers post to catalog products that they plan to purchase or would like to receive as gifts. These lists usually include the name of the list's owner and his or her city and state.

Using a couple of standard-issue PCs, Mr. Owad was able to download over 250,000 wish lists over the course of a day. He then searched the data for controversial or politically sensitive books and authors, from Kurt Vonnegut's *Slaughterhouse-Five* to the Koran. He then used Yahoo People Search to identify addresses and phone numbers for many of the list owners.

Mr. Owad ended up with maps of the United States showing the locations of people interested in particular books and ideas, including George Orwell's *1984*. He could just as easily have published a map showing the residences of people interested in books about treating depression or adopting a child. "It used to be," Mr. Owad concluded, "you had to get a warrant to monitor a person or a group of people. Today, it is increasingly easy to monitor ideas. And then track them back to people."

What Mr. Owad did by hand can increasingly be performed automatically, with data-mining software that draws from many sites and databases. One of the essential characteristics of the Net is the interconnection of diverse stores of information. The "openness" of databases is what gives the system much of its power and usefulness. But it also makes it easy to discover hidden relationships among far-flung bits of data.

In 2006, a team of scholars from the University of Minnesota described how easy it is for data-mining software to create detailed personal profiles of individuals—even when they post information anonymously. The software is based on a simple principle: People tend to leave lots of little pieces of information about themselves and their opinions in many different places on the Web. By identifying correspondences among the data, sophisticated algorithms can identify individuals with extraordinary precision. And it's not a big leap from there to discovering the people's names. The researchers noted that most Americans can be identified by name and address using only their zip code, birthday and gender—three pieces of information that people often divulge when they register at a website.

The more deeply the Net is woven into our work lives and leisure activities, the more exposed we become. Over the last few years, as social networking services have grown in popularity, people have come to entrust ever more intimate details about their lives to sites like Facebook and Twitter. The incorporation of GPS transmitters into cell phones and the rise of location-tracking services like Foursquare provide powerful tools for assembling moment-by-moment records of people's movements. As reading shifts from printed pages onto networked devices like the Kindle and the Nook, it becomes possible for companies to more closely monitor people's reading habits—even when they're not surfing the Web.

"You have zero privacy," Scott McNealy remarked back in 1999, when he was chief executive of Sun Microsystems. "Get over it." Other Silicon Valley CEOs have expressed similar sentiments in just the last few months. While Internet companies

Personal Information Online

Percentage of adult Internet users who say this information about them is available online.

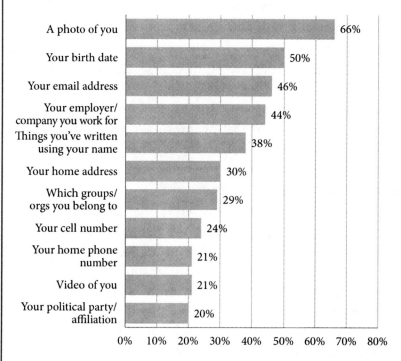

Source: Pew Research Center's Internet & American Life Project Omnibus Survey, conducted July 11–14, 2013, on landline and cell phones. N=792 for Internet users and smartphone owners. Interviews were conducted in English on landline and cell phones. The margin of error on the sample is +/– 3.8 percentage points.

TAKEN FROM: Pew Research Center, "Anonymity, Privacy, and Security Online," September 5, 2013.

may be complacent about the erosion of personal privacy—they, after all, profit from the trend—the rest of us should be wary. There are real dangers.

First and most obvious is the possibility that our personal data will fall into the wrong hands. Powerful data-mining tools are available not only to legitimate corporations and researchers, but also to crooks, con men and creeps. As more data about us is collected and shared online, the threats from unsanctioned interceptions of the data grow. Criminal syndicates can use purloined information about our identities to commit financial fraud, and stalkers can use locational data to track our whereabouts.

The first line of defense is, of course, common sense. We need to take personal responsibility for the information we share whenever we log on. But no amount of caution will protect us from the dispersal of information collected without our knowledge. If we're not aware of what data about us are available online, and how they're being used and exchanged, it can be difficult to guard against abuses.

A second danger is the possibility that personal information may be used to influence our behavior and even our thoughts in ways that are invisible to us. Personalization's evil twin is manipulation. As mathematicians and marketers refine data-mining algorithms, they gain more precise ways to predict people's behavior as well as how they'll react when they're presented with online ads and other digital stimuli. Just this past week, Google CEO Eric Schmidt acknowledged that by tracking a person's messages and movements, an algorithm can accurately predict where that person will go next.

As marketing pitches and product offerings become more tightly tied to our past patterns of behavior, they become more powerful as triggers of future behavior. Already, advertisers are able to infer extremely personal details about people by monitoring their Web-browsing habits. They can then use that knowledge to create ad campaigns customized to particular individuals. A man who visits a site about obesity, for instance, may soon see a lot of promotional messages related to weight-loss treatments. A woman who does research about anxiety may be bombarded with pharmaceutical ads. The line between personalization and manipulation is a fuzzy one, but one thing is certain: We can never know if the line has been crossed if we're unaware of what companies know about us.

Safeguarding privacy online isn't particularly hard. It requires that software makers and site operators assume that people want to keep their information private. Privacy settings should be on by default and easy to modify. And when companies track our behavior or use personal details to tailor messages, they should provide an easy way for us to see what they're doing.

The greatest danger posed by the continuing erosion of personal privacy is that it may lead us as a society to devalue the concept of privacy, to see it as outdated and unimportant. We may begin to see privacy merely as a barrier to efficient shopping and socializing. That would be a tragedy. As the computer security expert Bruce Schneier has observed, privacy is not just a screen we hide behind when we do something naughty or embarrassing; privacy is "intrinsic to the concept of liberty." When we feel that we're always being watched, we begin to lose our sense of self-reliance and free will and, along with it, our individuality. "We become children," writes Mr. Schneier, "fettered under watchful eyes."

Privacy is not only essential to life and liberty; it's essential to the pursuit of happiness, in the broadest and deepest sense. We human beings are not just social creatures; we're also private creatures. What we don't share is as important as what we do share. The way that we choose to define the boundary between our public self and our private self will vary greatly from person to person, which is exactly why it's so important to be ever vigilant in defending everyone's right to set that boundary as he or she sees fit.

"We need to be more honest about what we mean when we say we want to protect 'privacy' online."

No More Privacy Paranoia

Farhad Manjoo

In the following viewpoint, Farhad Manjoo argues that there is a danger of reacting to concern about online privacy in a manner that is too hasty and radical, citing a recent response to Google's privacy practices as risking this maximalist approach to online privacy. Manjoo cautions that the data collected online has many beneficial uses that people value and, as such, a more rational discussion about privacy is needed. Manjoo is a technology columnist for the New York Times *and the author of* True Enough: Learning to Live in a Post-Fact Society.

As you read, consider the following questions:

1. According to the author, in a privacy settlement with the Federal Trade Commission, Google agreed to privacy audits for how many years?

2. How has data collected by Google been used for public health, according to the author?

3. Manjoo cites what example in support of his claim that our actions about privacy contradict our stated concerns?

L ast week [March 30, 2011] the Federal Trade Commission [FTC] and Google signed a broad privacy settlement that requires the search company to submit to "privacy audits" every two years. The agreement ended a dispute that began last year, when Google launched Buzz, the ill-fated social-messaging system built into Gmail.

Audits for Google

According to the FTC, just about everything about Buzz was flawed. Google made it difficult for users to decline to join, or to leave after they'd joined (the "Turn off Buzz" button didn't actually turn off Buzz). Even if you wanted to participate, the service didn't make it clear how to keep your private information private (the earliest versions of the service made public a list of the people you e-mailed frequently). Most damningly, the FTC says that Buzz violated Google's own privacy policy. In that policy, Google promises that it will ask permission when it uses private information acquired for one product to produce something else. In this case, the FTC says, Google used information gathered for Gmail to build a social networking service that had nothing to do with e-mail. It never asked permission to do so. For all these sins, Google agreed to submit to a procedure that none of its rivals will have to endure—regular reviews of its privacy and data-collection practices by independent consultants. The audits will last for 20 years—that is, longer than the life span of many tech giants. Will there even be a "Web" to search in 2030?

Buzz was certainly a privacy boondoggle for Google—a black eye for a company that had been trying to position itself as the good guy to Facebook's bad guy. I agree with the FTC

"I deplore the lack of Internet privacy and so do 5,000 of my Facebook friends!" © Chris Wildt/CartoonStock.

that Google should pay for the mistakes it made (the company has apologized and says it's fixed its privacy procedures to prevent another such imbroglio). And if they're done judiciously, the privacy audits may prove helpful in ensuring that Google stays on the up and up.

But that's what I worry about: Will the audits in fact be done judiciously? There's a good chance that privacy regulators—spurred by a public that doesn't really know what it wants when it comes to online privacy—may go too far, blocking Google from collecting and analyzing information about its users. That will be a terrible outcome, because while we all reflexively hate the thought of a company analyzing our digital lives, we also benefit from this practice in many ways that we don't appreciate.

The Benefits of Data Collection

I know I sound naïve, but bear with me. Yes, Google collects a lot of information about all of us. It does so on purpose, and for all sorts of reasons. Some of these reasons we don't like very much—Google, like all big Web companies, sells ads, and it can get more money for those ads when they're targeted to you. This practice pays for the Web, and it's the reason you don't pay a fee to conduct a Google search. Still, I understand why people are wary of online data collection. Too often, though, our conversations about online privacy end right here.

Broadly speaking, there are two types of data that Web companies keep on us—personally identifiable information (like your name and list of friends), and information that can't be tied to you as an individual. In our discussions about privacy, we rarely make this important distinction. While we focus on the disadvantages of companies collecting our information, we rarely look at the innovations that wouldn't be possible without our personal data. This is especially true when it comes to anonymous data—information that can't be used to identify you, but which serves as the building blocks of amazing things.

Indeed, some of Google's best and most-loved products would not be possible without our data. Take the spell-checker: How does Google know you meant *Rebecca Black* when you typed *Rebeca Blacke?* Note that this is a trick that no ordinary, dictionary-based spell-checker could perform—these are proper nouns, and we're dealing with an ephemeral personality. But since Google has stored lots of other people's search requests for Black, it knows you're looking for the phenom behind "Friday." The theory behind the spell-checker can be applied more broadly. By studying words that often come together in search terms—for instance, people may either search for "los angeles *murder* rate" or "los angeles *homicide* rate"—

Google can detect that two completely different words may have the same meaning. This has profound implications for the future of computing: In a very real sense, mining search queries is teaching computers how to understand language (and not just English, either). If Google were forced to forget every search query right after it served up a result, none of these things would be possible.

The spell-checker is just one small example of what large-scale data mining makes possible. In my last column, I looked at another case—speech recognition, which relies on billions of audio samples and text queries to teach machines how to understand human speech. Here are some more: Google analyzes search logs to detect large-scale computer security threats; when it notices anomalous collections of searches (which viruses have been known to perform to seek out vulnerable Web servers) it can stop viruses in their tracks. Then there's "crowdsourced traffic." On many different smartphones, you can turn on a Google Maps feature called "My Location," which beams back anonymous data about where your phone is at any current moment. Google collects and analyzes this information to create real-time traffic reports on highways and even surface streets.

An even more important area of research is in prediction—by looking at what people are searching for today, Google can guess what's going to happen tomorrow or next month. In 2008, Google launched Flu Trends, a site that monitors increases in health-related searches in different parts of the world. The team behind the system published a research paper showing that they can accurately predict the outbreak of a flu epidemic in a certain region before public health authorities catch on to it. In 2009, Hal Varian, Google's chief economist, published a paper showing that Google searches can be used to predict a bevy of economic data, too, including retail sales and unemployment claims.

The Danger of Privacy Controls

There's something important to note about the spell-checker, Flu Trends, speech recognition, and other Google products based on data. They weren't planned. Google didn't begin saving search queries in order to build the spell-checker; it built the spell-checker because it began saving search queries, and eventually realized that the database could be useful. "You may not think of it right away—later on, you'll come up with some use for the data, and over the years we've constantly come up with new ways to look at data to improve our products and services," Varian told me.

This suggests the danger of our maximalist attitudes about online privacy. We all argue that we'd like companies to store less of our personal information and to jump through many hoops if it wants to store more. Members of Congress are now pushing for legislation that would tighten privacy controls at Web companies; there's even a move to expand the FTC's settlement with Google to all Web firms. I don't oppose greater privacy measures, so long as they're the product of an honest discussion. The trouble is we rarely have rational discussions about privacy. Witness the annual furor over Facebook: Every year or so, the media and activists get excited over some new and alarming slight by the social networking company. Yet our actions belie our concerns; while we all holler about how much we hate Facebook, none of us quit it—and, in fact, hundreds of thousands more keep signing up.

We need to be more honest about what we mean when we say we want to protect "privacy" online. Does this mean that we want to be able to control every single bread crumb we leave behind when we're on the Web? Many activists fear that the distinction between anonymous and personally identifiable data is eroding—that broad data-mining practices make it possible for Web companies to suss out who you are by analyzing supposedly "anonymous" data. Based on this worry, some regulators have proposed restrictions on the anonymous data that companies keep.

But if that's what we want to see happen, we ought to be clear about the costs. Yes, Web companies track a lot of what we do in our browsers. But the next time you misspell a word or get caught in a traffic jam or have your computer shut down by a virus, remember that tracking is not always a bad thing.

| "It is perfectly legal for companies to spy
on us, and it is very lucrative."

iSPY: How the Internet Buys and Sells Your Secrets

Jamie Bartlett

In the following viewpoint, Jamie Bartlett argues that personal data given online is sold by data brokers and used by companies, organizations, and politicians to target advertising, requests for donations, and messaging. Bartlett claims that this exchange of information for use of free Internet technology has gotten lopsided, where users are not privy to how their information may be used, and that there is a need for users to have greater control over their information. Bartlett is director of the Centre for the Analysis of Social Media at Demos, a think tank in Great Britain.

As you read, consider the following questions:

1. According to Bartlett, how many items of content do users upload to Facebook each week?

2. The author cites a survey that found what fraction of the population knows that mobile applications can collect personal data?

3. According to Bartlett, what does the German term *infor-mationelle Selbstbestimmung* mean?

You probably have no idea how much of yourself you have given away on the Internet, or how much it's worth. Never mind Big Brother, the all-seeing state; the real menace online is the Little Brothers—the companies who suck up your personal data, repackage it, then sell it to the highest bidder. The Little Brothers are answerable to no one, and they are everywhere.

What may seem innocuous, even worthless information—shopping, musical preferences, holiday destinations—is seized on by the digital scavengers who sift through cyberspace looking for information they can sell: a mobile phone number, a private e-mail address. The more respectable data-accumulating companies—Facebook, Google, Amazon—already have all that. Even donating money to charity by texting a word to a number means you can end up on databases as a 'giver'—and being inundated with phone calls from other noble causes. Once your details end up on a list, you can never quite control who will buy them.

As you surf the Web, thousands of 'third-party cookies' track your browsing habits. Then there's your smartphone, which can log information every waking and sleeping moment. Quintillions—yes, that really is a number—of pieces of data are being generated by us, about us. Look at Facebook. In a typical week, its users upload 20 billion items of content—pictures, names, preferences, shopping habits and other titbits: all information that can be stored and later employed to help advertisers.

It is perfectly legal for companies to spy on us, and it is very lucrative. Some analysts estimate we're each giving away up to £5,000 worth of data every year. A worldwide industry has emerged over the past decade that is dedicated to finding new ways of extracting and analysing this bounty. 'Data brokers' operate enormous clearinghouses which buy, analyse and then sell online and off-line data. One of the largest, Acxiom Corporation, is believed to hold information on about 500 million consumers around the world, and has annual sales of more than $1 billion. Many of the big social media companies, including Facebook, work closely with these data brokers—cross-referencing your status updates against post codes or loyalty-card data from shops. From thousands of fragments, they can build a remarkably detailed picture of you.

A little further down the chain, companies are scooping up your tweets or Facebook posts, analysing them and selling on the results for a hefty fee: This week Sony paid $200 million for a company that does exactly that. This doesn't just affect exhibitionists on Facebook; if you've completed the electoral register, your home address could be only a click away for anyone vaguely interested.

This harvested data can be used to figure out your probable location and guess at your consumer behaviour. In one infamous case, a US supermarket responded to a young female customer's purchases by offering her vouchers for various pregnancy products: These were intercepted by an unsuspecting and very irate father. In another, a GPS service designed to help drivers find quick routes was also selling the information to the Dutch police, who could use it to work out who was breaking local speed limits. Each year, the Little Brothers get cleverer.

This makes it easier than ever for companies—and even politicians—to pin you down with personalised and effective marketing, messages and offers. The Labour Party has recently hired one of Barack Obama's digital gurus, Matthew McGregor. Don't be surprised to see creepy targeted ads from Dave, Ed and Nick at the next general election, based on some innocuous comment you might have made on your Facebook page about wind farms.

The Collection of Data

Consumer data companies scoop up large amounts of consumer information about people around the world and sell it. . . .

They start with the basics, like names, addresses and contact information, and add on demographics, like age, race, occupation and "education level," according to consumer data firm Acxiom's overview of its various categories.

But that's just the beginning: The companies collect lists of people experiencing "life-event triggers" like getting married, buying a home, sending a kid to college—or even getting divorced.

Credit reporting giant Experian has a separate marketing services division, which sells lists of "names of expectant parents and families with newborns" that are "updated weekly."

The companies also collect data about your hobbies and many of the purchases you make. Want to buy a list of people who read romance novels? Epsilon can sell you that, as well as a list of people who donate to international aid charities.

Lois Beckett,
"Everything We Know About What Data Brokers
Know About You," ProPublica, June 13, 2014.

How worried should you be? Having slightly less irrelevant ads popping up on your screen hardly amounts to a sustained attack on your freedom. Data brokers can't break down your door. And after all, when you join a social network or run a search on Google, it's an exchange: You let people spy on you, and they give you an incredible service for free.

But this exchange is starting to become a bit one-sided. Every time we download an Internet app, we accept a lengthy list of terms and conditions. But few of us really know what we're signing up to—one recent survey found under half of us knew that mobile phone apps can collect and store personal data.

And those terms and conditions? They're usually comprehensible only to a contract lawyer with a background in software engineering, but we click yes and hope for the best. The results were explained well in a recent documentary, *Terms and Conditions May Apply*. 'The greatest heist in history wasn't about taking money,' says the voice-over. 'It was about taking your information—and you agreed to all of it.'

Agreement, in this case, means clicking 'OK' to the contracts that include all sorts of worrying, loosely worded clauses—and which it would take about a month of your life each year to read properly. But perhaps you should set that time aside. A British firm recently included a clause which asked for permission to 'claim, now and for evermore, your immortal soul'—a techie's joke which harvested 7,000 souls in one day.

When the hugely popular Instagram updated its user agreement to say that 'a business ... may pay us to display your photos ... without any compensation to you', uproar ensued, the clause was removed, and the company declared that it had never intended to sell any photos. But in order to opt out of data collection, or to object to nasty terms and conditions, you have to know exactly who's collecting your data—and it's hard to know where to start.

Civil liberties groups are increasingly concerned, because they realise that companies, police and governments have a mutual interest in the gathering of personal data. Nick Pickles, head of Big Brother Watch, says large-scale commercial data collection is a 'dream come true' for governments because it dramatically extends the possibility for surveillance. Intelligence agencies don't need to spy on you anymore: They can simply go to the relevant Internet companies and prise out of them what they need.

All this data is also a gold mine for fraudsters. Identity theft is increasing, which is no surprise, seeing how much information people post about themselves online. Often we're complicit. In saying where we are on our social media accounts, we also say where we are not. The website please robme.com is a joke—but it has a serious point behind it, a rather brutal reminder of the dangers of location-sharing online.

The Internet, of course, is just getting started. More and more everyday objects are being fitted with microchips: fridges, keys, wallets, cars. And even hair: Sony recently filed a patent for a SmartWig that could take photos and vibrate when you receive a message. Google's augmented reality glasses will be able to record what and who you're seeing. On a more mundane level, smart energy meters which can record your energy consumption patterns will be installed in every home by 2020. As it stands, no one really knows who will own all this information, and how it will be regulated.

The public is getting worried. So what should we do? The past six months have seen a flurry of 'crypto-parties'—free workshops to learn about how to protect your privacy online. (I attended a packed event last weekend in London.) Anonymous browsers like 'TOR', often used to access the 'dark net', are becoming more popular. The dark net is usually referred to as an online underworld where drugs, pornography and worse are bought and sold—but it's also one of the few places you can go to escape Brothers Little and Big. Even Facebook users who were once happy to share everything are tightening their privacy settings.

Here is another danger. It's right that people should be able to keep things private, but the vitality of the Internet depends on people sharing information: that was the whole point of the net when it began as an academic project in the late 1960s. The more you share, the more you receive. And there are many beneficial uses of data. Professor Nigel Shadbolt, director of the Open Data Institute, says that Google has been extremely successful at using search terms to understand how epidemics spread. Satnav [satellite navigation] technology is getting better at avoiding traffic jams, because of drivers agreeing to share their progress. Analysing our energy consumption patterns could cut down bills dramatically.

As director of the Centre for the Analysis of Social Media, I am dedicated to making this a serious discipline. Professor Shadbolt thinks if we can analyse the use of social media while respecting privacy and consent, the benefits to British society could be immense.

The digital revolution has transformed our lives, but the technology that does so much for us comes at a cost. For good or ill, the Internet has ravaged notions of privacy: It's not really possible to get by in the modern world without sharing information about yourself. The question is how to control that.

The Germans already have a term, *informationelle Selbstbestimmung*, which translates into knowing what data you have and being in control over how it's used. In part, that means us wising up to exactly what data is being sucked out of us. It also requires companies to be transparent about what data they're sucking—and how they'll use it. At the moment it's still too shadowy and confusing. Basic market competition should help. As the value of our personal information grows (and we become more aware of that value), companies that are open about what they're using will have a significant advantage over competitors. The big players are already looking for ways to give users more control over their data: even Acxiom has started to open up a little. It makes good business sense, and probably helps that politicians and quangos on both sides of the Atlantic have started to pay more attention to this issue.

But it may be that we do not want the Little Brothers to stop watching us entirely—we've become dependent on the services they help to deliver so cheaply. One of the reasons firms like Amazon and Google have grown so huge is that they deliver services which billions of us want. The majority of Brits now use Facebook, Twitter, Instagram or another social media account—none of which charge us a penny. As the saying goes: If you're not paying, you're the product.

> "While many debates over technology
> and privacy concern obscurity, the term
> rarely gets used."

Obscurity in Using Technology Is More Important than Privacy

Woodrow Hartzog and Evan Selinger

In the following viewpoint, Woodrow Hartzog and Evan Selinger argue that many of the debates about technology and privacy are actually about obscurity. Hartzog and Selinger contend that the desire for obscurity often forms a better framework for understanding concerns about online information. Hartzog is an assistant professor at Samford University's Cumberland School of Law and an affiliate scholar at the Center for Internet and Society at Stanford Law School. Selinger is an associate professor of philosophy at Rochester Institute of Technology and a fellow at the Institute for Ethics and Emerging Technologies.

As you read, consider the following questions:

1. How do the authors define the idea of obscurity?

2. How do the authors describe the "you choose who to let in" narrative about online privacy?

3. What example do the authors give to illustrate how well-intentioned searches on Facebook's Graph Search tool can be problematic?

Facebook's announcement of its new Graph Search tool on Tuesday [January 15, 2013] set off yet another round of rapid-fire analysis about whether Facebook is properly handling its users' privacy. Unfortunately, most of the rapid-fire analysts haven't framed the story properly. Yes, [Mark] Zuckerberg appears to be respecting our current privacy settings. And, yes, there just might be more stalking ahead. Neither framing device, however, is adequate. If we rely too much on them, we'll miss the core problem: The more accessible our Facebook information becomes, the less obscurity protects our interests.

The Concept of Obscurity

While many debates over technology and privacy concern obscurity, the term rarely gets used. This is unfortunate, as "privacy" is an overextended concept. It grabs our attention easily, but is hard to pin down. Sometimes, people talk about privacy when they are worried about confidentiality. Other times they evoke privacy to discuss issues associated with corporate access to personal information. Fortunately, obscurity has a narrower purview.

Obscurity is the idea that when information is hard to obtain or understand, it is, to some degree, safe. Safety, here, doesn't mean inaccessible. Competent and determined data hunters armed with the right tools can always find a way to get it. Less committed folks, however, experience great effort as a deterrent.

Online, obscurity is created through a combination of factors. Being invisible to search engines increases obscurity. So does using privacy settings and pseudonyms. Disclosing information in coded ways that only a limited audience will grasp enhances obscurity, too. Since few online disclosures are truly confidential or highly publicized, the lion's share of communication on the social web falls along the expansive continuum of obscurity: a range that runs from completely hidden to totally obvious.

Legal debates surrounding obscurity can be traced back at least to *U.S. Department of Justice v. Reporters Committee for Freedom of the Press* (1989). In this decision, the United States Supreme Court recognized a privacy interest in the "practical obscurity" of information that was technically available to the public, but could only be found by spending a burdensome and unrealistic amount of time and effort in obtaining it. Since this decision, discussion of obscurity in the case law remains sparse. Consequently, the concept remains under-theorized as courts continue their seemingly Sisyphean struggle [a never-ending struggle] with finding meaning in the concept of privacy.

Privacy and Obscurity

Many contemporary privacy disputes are probably better classified as concern over losing obscurity. Consider the recent debate over whether a newspaper violated the privacy rights of gun owners by publishing a map comprised of information gleaned from public records. The situation left many scratching their heads. After all, how can public records be considered private? What obscurity draws our attention to is that while the records were accessible to any member of the public prior to the rise of big data, more effort was required to obtain, aggregate, and publish them. In that prior context, technological constraints implicitly protected privacy interests. Now, in an attempt to keep pace with diminishing structural barriers, New York is considering excepting gun owners from [according to Abby Rogers] "public records laws that normally allow newspapers or private citizens access to certain information the government collects."

The obscurity of public records and other legally available information is at issue in recent disputes over publishing mug shots and homeowner defaults. Likewise, claims for "privacy in public," as occur in discussion over license-plate readers, GPS [global positioning system] trackers, and facial-recognition technologies, are often pleas for obscurity that get either miscommunicated or misinterpreted as insistence that one's public interactions should remain secret.

Obscurity received some attention when Facebook previously rolled out Timeline. The Electronic Privacy Information Center, for example, was dismayed by how easy the design made it to retrieve past posts—including ones that previously required extensive manual searching to locate.

Two Narratives

Alas, the two dominant ways of discussing Graph have not had that same focus on obscurity. One narrative suggests that since Graph will only reveal information to users that was previously visible to them or publicly shared, it presents no new privacy issues. As Facebook hammered home, a user's original privacy settings are neither altered nor violated. According to Kashmir Hill, "Zuckerberg and crew emphasized the 'privacy awareness' of the new search engine."

Respecting Facebook users' privacy settings is no small feature, due to the harm that can result when privacy settings are given too little weight in socio-technical design. Thanks to the soothing message and intuitive appeal of the "self-selected insiders" narrative, many reporters are spreading its gospel. *Wired* and CNN, among others, note Graph doesn't expose any information that wasn't already available on Facebook.

Ultimately, the "you choose who to let in" narrative is powerful because it trades on traditional notions of space and boundary regulation, and further appeals to our heightened sense of individual responsibility, and, possibly even vanity. The basic message is that so long as we exercise good judgment when selecting our friends, no privacy problems will arise. What this appeal to status quo relations and existing privacy settings conceals is the transformative potential of Graph: New types of searching can emerge that, due to enhanced frequency and newly created associations between data points, weaken, and possibly obliterate, obscurity. Of course, that result won't bother everyone. Some users won't miss their obscurity havens, while others will find the change dismaying. As we'll clarify shortly, those who become dismayed will have good reason for being upset.

The other dominant narrative emerging is that Graph will simplify "stalking." Kashmir Hill states, "Good news for snoops: the new tool will make Facebook stalking much easier." Megan Rose Dickey wrote an article titled "Facebook's Graph Search Is Awesome for Stalkers and Hookups." While utilization of the "stalker" frame brings us a little closer to articulating what the harm from Graph might be, it, too, is inadequate.

The Problem with the Stalking Frame

First, the stalking frame risks creating undue psychological associations with the more severe harms of stalking, as legally defined and prohibited. Yes, we recognize these accounts use "stalking" colloquially. But words have power, and such deliberatively evocative rhetoric unduly muddies the already murky conceptual waters.

Second, because of this, the stalker frame muddies the concept, implying that the problem is people with bad intentions getting our information. Determined stalkers certainly pose a threat to the obscurity of information because they represent an increased likelihood that obscure information will be found and understood. Stalkers seek and collect information with varying degrees of rigor. But as social search moves from an atomistic to composite form, many harms resulting from loss of obscurity will likely be accidental. Well-intentioned searches can be problematic, too.

Consider the following hypothetical to demonstrate this point. Mark Zuckerberg mentioned that Graph is still in beta and many new features could be added down the road. It is not a stretch to assume Graph could enable searching through the content of posts a user has liked or commented on and generating categories of interests from it. For example, users could search which of their friends are interested in politics, or, perhaps, specifically, in left-wing politics. While many Facebook users are outspoken on politics, others hold these beliefs close. For various reasons, these less outspoken users might still support the political causes of their friends through likes and comments, but refrain from posting political material themselves. In this scenario, a user who wasn't a fan of political groups or causes, didn't list political groups or causes as interests, and didn't post political stories, could still be identified as political. Graph would wrench these scattered showings of support from the various corners of Facebook into a composite profile that presents both obscurity and accuracy concerns.

The final reason the stalker frame is not a good fit for Graph is that it implies the harm at stake is the experience of feeling "creeped out." While the term 'creepy' isn't appearing as much as with other Facebook-related stories, it is still a nontrivial aspect of the Graph narrative. As one of us has previously posited, due to its vagueness and heightened emotional resonance, 'creepy' is not a helpful term to use when identifying the harm that might result from new technologies.

The Debate About Technology

Some of the chatter about Graph and privacy belies the optimistic belief that Facebook will not diminish too much obscurity in order to keep consumers happy and willing to post their lives away. Facebook regularly emphasizes the importance of users believing that posting on Facebook is safe. But is it really wise to presume Facebook's financial interests align with the user interest in maintaining obscurity? In a system that purportedly relies upon user control, it is still unclear how and if users will be able to detect when their personal information is no longer obscure. How will they be able to anticipate the numerous different queries that might expose previously obscure information? Will users even be aware of all of the composite results including their information?

Accurately targeting the potential harms and interests at stake is only the first step in the debate about Graph and other similar technologies. Obscurity is a protective state that can further a number of goals, such as autonomy, self-fulfillment, socialization, and relative freedom from the abuse of power. A major task ahead is for society to determine how much obscurity citizens need to thrive.

Periodical and Internet Sources Bibliography

The following articles have been selected to supplement the diverse views presented in this chapter.

Eva Galperin and Jillian C. York	"Yes, Online Privacy Really Is Possible," *Slate*, February 14, 2014.
Doug Gross	"How Your Movements Create a GPS 'Fingerprint,'" CNN, March 26, 2013.
Jim Harper	"*U.S. v. Jones*: A Big Privacy Win," *Cato at Liberty*, January 23, 2012.
John Hendel	"Why Journalists Shouldn't Fear Europe's 'Right to Be Forgotten,'" *Atlantic*, January 25, 2012.
Marcia Hofmann, Rainey Reitman, and Cindy Cohn	"When the Government Comes Knocking, Who Has Your Back?," Electronic Frontier Foundation, May 31, 2012.
Alexis C. Madrigal	"I'm Being Followed: How Google—and 104 Other Companies—Are Tracking Me on the Web," *Atlantic*, February 29, 2012.
Ellen Messmer	"Want Security, Privacy? Turn Off That Smartphone, Tablet GPS," Network World, August 21, 2012.
Rebecca J. Rosen	"Why the *Jones* Supreme Court Ruling on GPS Tracking Is Worse than It Sounds," *Atlantic*, January 23, 2012.
Jeffrey Toobin	"The Solace of Oblivion: In Europe, the Right to Be Forgotten Trumps the Internet," *New Yorker*, September 29, 2014.
John Villasenor	"In the Mobile Ecosystem, Privacy Is an Endangered Right," *Globe and Mail*, January 24, 2012.

OPPOSING
VIEWPOINTS®
SERIES

CHAPTER 2

Do Security Measures Infringe on Privacy Rights?

Chapter Preface

Documents released by former National Security Agency (NSA) contractor Edward Snowden in spring 2013 suggest that the NSA has engaged in surveillance of Americans and foreigners. The news of such widespread surveillance created controversy both within and outside the United States. What is at issue is not simply a question of privacy rights alone, but the extent to which privacy rights can be outweighed by national security concerns.

American opinion on NSA surveillance and privacy is varied—even conflicting—depending on the questions asked. According to a June 2013 poll by the Pew Research Center and the *Washington Post*, a majority of Americans—56 percent—said that "tracking the telephone records of millions of Americans is an acceptable way for the NSA to investigate terrorism," though a sizeable minority—41 percent—said it was unacceptable. When asked if it was acceptable for government to monitor everyone's e-mail to prevent possible terrorism, 45 percent assented, whereas a majority—52 percent—disagreed. Getting slightly different results, a Gallup poll conducted that same month found that only 37 percent of adults approved of the federal government obtaining records from US telephone and Internet companies to "compile telephone call logs and Internet communications." The poll found that 53 percent of respondents disagreed with the government activity when worded in this way. In July 2013, the Pew Research Center reported that different question wording produced different responses on the issue of government surveillance: Mentioning antiterrorism elicited more support for the programs, whereas mentioning neither terrorism nor court approval led to high opposition.

When the question was specifically about balancing security and privacy, the results were less evenly divided: 62 percent of those surveyed said it was more important for government to investigate terrorism than to avoid intruding on privacy. A *Washington Post*–ABC News poll in July 2013 obtained similar results, with 59 percent assenting to the view that it was more important for the federal government to investigate possible terrorist threats, even if that intruded on personal privacy. That poll found that almost three-quarters of Americans believed that surveillance of telephone call records and Internet traffic certainly does intrude on some Americans' privacy rights. Nonetheless, even among the majority who said this, 39 percent of them said that such intrusions were justified.

A Pew Research Center survey in January 2014 found that support for the government's collection of telephone and Internet data "as part of anti-terrorism efforts" had fallen: 53 percent expressed disapproval and only 40 percent expressed approval. Almost half of the respondents were concerned that there are not adequate limits on what telephone and Internet data the government can collect. As the authors of the viewpoints in this chapter illustrate, there is wide disagreement about the extent to which privacy ought to be rightly foregone in the name of national security and to what extent government should be limited on intelligence gathering for this purpose.

| "We need to recognize that security is more important than surveillance."

NSA Surveillance Threatens Privacy and Security

Bruce Schneier

In the following viewpoint, Bruce Schneier argues that the surveillance state in the United States is strong, covert, and involves several government agencies. Schneier contends that not only is surveillance not an effective means of ensuring security, but it also has high financial and social costs, with a propensity for abuse. Schneier concludes that a simple legal fix will not solve the problem. Schneier is a security technologist and the author of Liars and Outliers: Enabling the Trust That Society Needs to Thrive.

As you read, consider the following questions:

1. Schneier claims that the NSA collect-everything mentality is a holdover from what era?

2. The author gives what five examples of episodes where surveillance was, or would have been, abused?

3. Schneier contends that securing the Internet requires what in addition to laws?

Secret NSA [National Security Agency] eavesdropping is still in the news. Details about once-secret programs continue to leak. The director of national intelligence has recently declassified additional information, and the president's review group has just released its report and recommendations.

The Surveillance State

With all of this going on, it's easy to become inured to the breadth and depth of the NSA's activities. But through the disclosures, we've learned an enormous amount about the agency's capabilities, how it is failing to protect us, and what we need to do to regain security in the Information Age.

First and foremost, the surveillance state is robust. It is robust politically, legally, and technically. I can name three different NSA programs to collect Gmail user data. These programs are based on three different technical eavesdropping capabilities. They rely on three different legal authorities. They involve collaborations with three different companies. And this is just Gmail. The same is true for cell phone call records, Internet chats, and cell phone location data.

Second, the NSA continues to lie about its capabilities. It hides behind tortured interpretations of words like "collect," "incidentally," "target," and "directed." It cloaks programs in multiple code names to obscure their full extent and capabilities. Officials testify that a particular surveillance activity is not done under one particular program or authority, conveniently omitting that it is done under some other program or authority.

Third, U.S. government surveillance is not just about the NSA. The [Edward] Snowden documents have given us extraordinary details about the NSA's activities, but we now know that the CIA [Central Intelligence Agency], NRO [National Reconnaissance Office], FBI [Federal Bureau of Investigation], DEA [Drug Enforcement Administration], and local police all engage in ubiquitous surveillance using the same sorts of eavesdropping tools, and that they regularly share information with each other.

The Effectiveness of Surveillance

The NSA's collect-everything mentality is largely a holdover from the Cold War, when a voyeuristic interest in the Soviet Union was the norm. Still, it is unclear how effective targeted surveillance against "enemy" countries really is. Even when we learn actual secrets, as we did regarding Syria's use of chemical weapons earlier this year, we often can't do anything with the information.

Ubiquitous surveillance should have died with the fall of communism, but it got a new—and even more dangerous— life with the intelligence community's post-9/11 [referring to the September 11, 2001, terrorist attacks on the United States] "never again" terrorism mission. This quixotic goal of preventing something from happening forces us to try to know everything that does happen. This pushes the NSA to eavesdrop on online gaming worlds and on every cell phone in the world. But it's a fool's errand; there are simply too many ways to communicate.

We have no evidence that any of this surveillance makes us safer. NSA director general Keith Alexander responded to these stories in June by claiming that he disrupted 54 terrorist plots. In October, he revised that number downward to 13, and then to "one or two." At this point, the only "plot" prevented was that of a San Diego man sending $8,500 to support a Somali militant group. We have been repeatedly told that these surveillance programs would have been able to stop 9/11, yet the NSA didn't detect the Boston bombings—even though one of the two terrorists was on the watch list and the

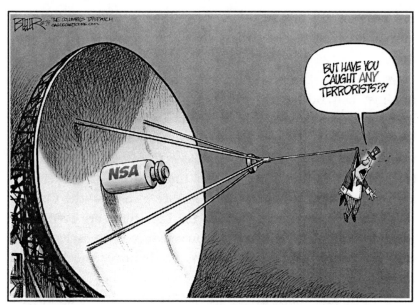

Caught by the NSA © Nate Beeler/Political Cartoons.com.

other had a sloppy social media trail. Bulk collection of data and metadata is an ineffective counterterrorism tool.

The Negative Effects of Surveillance

Not only is ubiquitous surveillance ineffective, it is extraordinarily costly. I don't mean just the budgets, which will continue to skyrocket. Or the diplomatic costs, as country after country learns of our surveillance programs against their citizens. I'm also talking about the cost to our society. It breaks so much of what our society has built. It breaks our political systems, as Congress is unable to provide any meaningful oversight, and citizens are kept in the dark about what government does. It breaks our legal systems, as laws are ignored or reinterpreted, and people are unable to challenge government actions in court. It breaks our commercial systems, as U.S. computer products and services are no longer trusted worldwide. It breaks our technical systems, as the very protocols of the Internet become untrusted. And it breaks our social systems; the loss of privacy, freedom, and liberty is much more damaging to our society than the occasional act of random violence.

And finally, these systems are susceptible to abuse. This is not just a hypothetical problem. Recent history illustrates many episodes where this information was, or would have been, abused: [J. Edgar] Hoover and his FBI spying, [Senator Joseph] McCarthy [and his search for Communist sympathizers], Martin Luther King Jr. and the civil rights movement, antiwar Vietnam protesters, and—more recently—the Occupy [Wall Street] movement. Outside the U.S., there are even more extreme examples. Building the surveillance state makes it too easy for people and organizations to slip over the line into abuse.

It's not just domestic abuse we have to worry about; it's the rest of the world, too. The more we choose to eavesdrop on the Internet and other communications technologies, the less we are secure from eavesdropping by others. Our choice isn't between a digital world where the NSA can eavesdrop and one where the NSA is prevented from eavesdropping; it's between a digital world that is vulnerable to all attackers, and one that is secure for all users.

The Need to Limit Surveillance

Fixing this problem is going to be hard. We are long past the point where simple legal interventions can help. The bill in Congress to limit NSA surveillance won't actually do much to limit NSA surveillance. Maybe the NSA will figure out an interpretation of the law that will allow it to do what it wants anyway. Maybe it'll do it another way, using another justification. Maybe the FBI will do it and give it a copy. And when asked, it'll lie about it.

NSA-level surveillance is like the Maginot Line [concrete obstacles between the border of France and Germany during the 1930s] was in the years before World War II: ineffective and wasteful. We need to openly disclose what surveillance we have been doing, and the known insecurities that make it possible. We need to work toward security, even if other countries like China continue to use the Internet as a giant surveillance platform. We need to build a coalition of free-world nations dedicated to a secure global Internet, and we need to continually push back against bad actors—both state and non-state—that work against that goal.

Securing the Internet requires both laws and technology. It requires Internet technology that secures data wherever it is and however it travels. It requires broad laws that put security ahead of both domestic and international surveillance. It requires additional technology to enforce those laws, and a worldwide enforcement regime to deal with bad actors. It's not easy, and has all the problems that other international issues have: nuclear, chemical, and biological weapon nonproliferation; small arms trafficking; human trafficking; money laundering; intellectual property. Global information security and anti-surveillance needs to join those difficult global problems, so we can start making progress.

The president's review group recommendations are largely positive, but they don't go nearly far enough. We need to recognize that security is more important than surveillance, and work toward that goal.

> *"If anything, the intelligence community is far more careful with the data it collects about Americans than are Google, Amazon, and Facebook."*

Privacy Concerns About NSA Intelligence Gathering Are Unfounded

Gary Schmitt

In the following viewpoint, Gary Schmitt argues that recent concerns about data collection practices of the American intelligence community are not warranted. Schmitt contends that actions by the National Security Agency (NSA) and the Federal Bureau of Investigation (FBI) are closely monitored and, therefore, unlikely to violate privacy in an egregious manner. Schmitt is the codirector of the Marilyn Ware Center for Security Studies at the American Enterprise Institute (AEI) and the director of AEI's Program on American Citizenship.

As you read, consider the following questions:

1. According to the author, has there been an increase or a decrease in the use of national security letters recently?

2. What National Security Agency (NSA) activity is protected by the Fourth Amendment to the US Constitution, according to Schmitt?

3. What examples does the author give of previous times in history when the balance between safety and liberty was more problematic than now?

In the wake of all the "leaks" by Edward Snowden of the National Security Agency's [NSA's] collection programs and the resulting debate over those programs, one constantly hears from elected officials and the commentariat about the need to strike the right balance between privacy and security. More often than not, this is followed by a suggestion that, as a country, since 9/11 [referring to the September 11, 2001, terrorist attacks on the United States], we haven't. Putting aside for the moment that no one has come up with evidence that the NSA, in spite of all the powerful capabilities it has at hand, has done anything untoward, the common refrain is that we are only a step away from the era of "Big Brother."

The Intelligence Community

Yet anyone who knows anything about the modern American intelligence community knows that it is virtually impossible for any of its major components to carry out a program significantly impinging on American privacy and get away with it for any extended period. Between the agencies' own inspector generals, the oversight provided by the courts, Congress, and the executive departments and agencies themselves, any effort to stray outside the lines is not likely to go undetected or unreported for very long.

A telling example is the FBI's [Federal Bureau of Investigation's] expansive use of "national security letters" [NSLs], administrative subpoenas used by the bureau to obtain transactional information from third parties—such as credit card information, travel history, etc. Under the [USA]

PATRIOT Act, the FBI was given more discretion to employ NSLs in connection with counterterrorism investigations. In short order, having been blamed in part for not preventing 9/11, the bureau took advantage of the new provisions and greatly expanded its NSL requests. But this hardly went unnoticed. Congress, the courts, and internal FBI and Justice Department auditors all weighed in to impose greater rigor on how this investigative tool was used, with the result that the number of NSLs has decreased, oversight has been beefed up and, with the president's most recent directive, greater transparency ordered in their use.

Moreover, the worry that the intelligence community will become a "rogue" entity ignores the undeniable fact that there are intelligence community employees who would probably not hesitate to go public if they really thought American liberties were being threatened. While there are always "go along, get along" individuals in any bureaucracy, since the mid-[19]70s, intelligence officials know crossing such lines will almost certainly lead to more trouble than it's worth, either to them or their agencies.

The Complexity of Privacy

Part of the problem—indeed, a key problem in the debate—is that we have subsumed civil liberties under the expansive banner of "privacy" and ignored just how complex the notion of privacy is in today's world. When talking about civil liberties, it is well to remind ourselves that the kind of judicially authorized telephony data that NSA collects and that we are arguing about (numbers dialed and time stamps, but not content) has long been held by the courts not to violate the 4th Amendment's proscription against "unreasonable searches" by the government. Nor have any of our other core liberties—such as freedom of the press, religion, conscience and association, the right to vote, the right to move from state to state, and, yes, the right to bear arms—been undermined in any real

NSA Surveillance

NSA [National Security Agency] handles data with a lot more care and supervision than Facebook or Google. Out of the thousands of NSA employees, for example, the phone database is handled by 22 technicians, and far from being deathly secret, their operating procedure is transparent, even ... banal. Algorithms sift through mountains of phone calls, including overseas calls, matching phone numbers to numbers with known terrorist links. Only when the technician can show one of seven superiors "a reasonable, articulable suspicion" that the number could be linked to a terrorist network is he or she allowed to pull up the dates of calls made and received over five years, the other parties' phone numbers, and the durations of the calls—and nothing else.

Arthur Herman and John Yoo,
"A Defense of Bulk Surveillance: The NSA Programs
Enhance Security Without Uniquely Compromising Privacy,"
National Review, vol. 66, no. 6, April 7, 2014.

way by the government or its intelligence agencies since 9/11. If anything, other than the aggravation of airport screening and tightened border controls, Americans are just as free today as they were on September 10, 2001.

Privacy is a different matter. Americans want privacy in theory but give it away to all kinds of entities on a daily basis when they use the Internet for buying books or movie tickets, search the Internet for this or that, post their daily affairs on social media, or even commute to work using an E-ZPass which, while it allows John Doe the convenience of bypassing long lines at the toll plaza, records precisely when his car was on a certain stretch of highway and can be preserved in a searchable form, *ad infinitum*. If anything, the intelligence community is far more careful with the data it collects about Americans than are Google, Amazon, and Facebook.

Because we've lost sight of what our core civil liberties are, we tend to forget those periods in American history where getting the balance between safety and liberty was far more difficult and problematic than it is today. During previous wars, American presidents have suspended the writ of habeas corpus, ignored the authority of the courts, censored publications, compromised mail, and interned over a hundred thousand Japanese immigrants and Japanese-American citizens in "war relocation camps." We're nowhere near that state today.

It was all well and good that in his speech on January 17 [2014], the president said that "throughout American history, intelligence has helped secure our country and freedom." That's certainly true. But when President [Barack] Obama then went on to offer up the "cautionary tale" of East Germany, where "vast unchecked surveillance turned citizens into informers and persecuted people for what they said in the privacy of their own homes," he fed a fear among the American public that is neither responsible nor warranted by reality.

"We need to set aside the rhetoric of privacy and focus instead on creating genuine safeguards against the abuse of government power."

Privacy Is a Red Herring: The Debate Over NSA Surveillance Is About Something Else Entirely

Rosa Brooks

In the following viewpoint, Rosa Brooks argues that the concerns about privacy are frequently about safety from harm. Brooks contends that governmental concern for privacy is about maintaining secrecy to avoid harm. She claims that individual concern for privacy is often about desiring freedom from harm; with respect to concerns about government surveillance, she says the worry is that governmental power might be used in an abusive manner. Brooks is a law professor at Georgetown University and a senior fellow at the New America Foundation.

As you read, consider the following questions:

1. According to Brooks, defenders of mass surveillance by the National Security Agency (NSA) insist upon what?

2. In what way does the author say that government and its critics are often suspicious of claims of privacy and secrecy?

3. What is the essential difference between the privacy of governments and the privacy of individuals, according to Brooks?

There are curious parallels in the arguments made by those on opposing sides of debates about covert action and NSA surveillance. Both sides deploy the language of secrecy and privacy, but often do so in sloppy and contradictory ways.

Thus, responding to those outraged by recent revelations of mass surveillance, many NSA defenders insist, in effect, that those who have nothing to hide have nothing to fear. Stunned to discover that U.S. intelligence agencies have been "invading your privacy" by monitoring your email, web searches, and telephone records? Calm down: If you're not doing anything that threatens U.S. national security, no one at the NSA will be interested in you. Conversely, if you're one of those people determined to cover your online tracks—by using Tor, for example—don't be shocked if the intelligence community begins to view you with suspicion. Why would you work so hard to keep your activities secret from your own government, unless you're up to no good?

Many *critics* of covert intelligence agency activities take a remarkably similar line in response to government outrage over the leaking of secret NSA documents. If the NSA *isn't* doing anything illegal or immoral—such as invading the privacy of ordinary Americans or allied heads of state—then there's no need for all the secrecy. Why would the NSA stamp "top secret" on everything—and scream so loudly when classified documents are leaked—if it's *not* trying to hide something from the American public? Didn't Edward Snowden's leaks demonstrate that the NSA really *was* hiding unlawful behavior under the cloak of secrecy?

At the same time, both government actors and individuals are quick to demand that their own privacy must be respected. NSA activities inappropriately "violate people's privacy," says Google's Eric Schmidt. They constitute an "astonishing invasion of Americans' privacy," laments the ACLU [American Civil Liberties Union]. Rand Paul agrees: NSA monitoring is an "extraordinary invasion of privacy."

When the U.S. government decries leaks of "classified information," it too is invoking the concept of privacy: Secrecy is the privacy of governments. Just like individuals, governments value (and, up to a point, *need*) the right to be left alone. In order to function, governments sometimes need to operate out of the public eye. Effective diplomats may need to take different approaches with different states. Government employees need to know that they can speak candidly to one another without fear that every conversation will be reported on Twitter.

What a muddle. On the one hand, both individuals and governments insist on the importance of their right to "privacy." At the very same time, both government actors and their critics tend to be suspicious of claims of privacy and secrecy: Why would anyone *need* secrecy if they're doing nothing wrong?

These contradictory attitudes reflect a persistent and widely shared tendency to use the term "privacy" to cover a variety of quite different (and sometimes contradictory) things. As George Washington University Law School professor Daniel Solove puts it, privacy is "a concept in disarray. Nobody can articulate what it means." Ask a dozen people to define privacy and you'll get a dozen different answers: Privacy encompasses, notes Solove, "freedom of thought, control over one's body, solitude in one's home, control over personal information, freedom from surveillance, protection of one's reputation, and protection from searches and interrogations."

I'd add one more item to Solove's list of definitions: When people speak of privacy, often what they're *really* concerned about is not privacy at all, but very concrete kinds of economic and physical harm: job loss, theft, injury, imprisonment, and even death. That is: When people speak of privacy they're often speaking—albeit indirectly—about power, and its uses and abuses.

This becomes more evident when we push past the surface of claims about privacy.

It's impossible, of course, for either individuals or governments to possess total privacy. Our lives and actions are porous. We all know that a great deal of our "personal" information is "out there" and available to anyone willing to put in even a modicum of effort. Our neighbors can peek through our windows; strangers in cafes and on the Metro can listen in on our conversations and telephone calls; our Match.com dates can Google us—and that's nothing compared to the data compiled about us by marketers. For the most part, this doesn't trouble us—most of us simply accept it as the price of living in human society.

This is true for governments as well. You can put a "top secret" stamp on everything from lunch menus to NSA memos, but people still gossip, leave sensitive papers lying around, and speak indiscreetly to their spouses and friends— and there is always a journalist or spy hanging around who can put together loose scraps of information. What's more, building strong relationships sometimes *requires* disclosure of secret information: Just as friendships and love relationships are cemented by the sharing of intimate information, governments often find that building relationships with allies, journalists, congressional staffers, and think tanks requires at least some willingness to share "classified" information.

We know all this. Even so, we still bridle when we discover that the universe of people aware of our "private" information has unexpectedly expanded, or that the information we *knew* to be accessible has *in fact* been accessed.

It's one thing to know, in the abstract, that anyone walking by your house can see into your kitchen window, but it's another thing altogether to look out the kitchen window and discover someone staring fixedly at you. It's one thing to know that the soccer mom sitting one table over at Starbucks can probably make out the words on your laptop screen; it's another thing altogether to know that "the government" can do the same thing.

For government officials, it's one thing to know that NSA surveillance capabilities are, if not fully known, guessed at with substantial accuracy by everyone from journalists to Angela Merkel to al Qaeda operatives; it's another thing altogether to find classified memos describing those capabilities splashed all over the front page of the *Washington Post*.

But it's important to push ourselves to articulate just *why* individuals and governments are troubled when the circle of those with knowledge about them expands. Put differently, it's worth asking: When we talk about invasion of privacy, what are we really worried about?

From the government's perspective, the answer is usually straightforward: Governmental privacy—secrecy—isn't valuable in and of itself. It's valuable solely because it reduces the risk of certain harms. Secrecy about NSA capabilities reduces the likelihood that terrorists or other adversaries will find ways to evade NSA scrutiny, which increases the likelihood that the United States will be able to learn about potential threats early enough to thwart planned attacks.

On an individual level, many people find it more difficult to articulate why they're bothered by "invasions of privacy." But when you push hard enough, most people articulate a fear that isn't about that mushy concept we refer to as "privacy," but is in fact about similarly concrete issues of safety and freedom from harm. The man staring fixedly through our kitchen window bothers us not because we think he might discover us doing something "secret," but because he has violated norms of socially acceptable behavior in a way that makes him unpredictable: If he's willing to violate norms against staring, what other norms might he also violate? Will he become a stalker, a blackmailer, a burglar, a rapist, a murderer?

At bottom, something similar is true of typical public reactions to NSA surveillance. We may speak of "privacy," but what frightens most of us is not the abstract notion that "the government" might be "watching us"; rather, it is the very concrete possibility that information about us will be misconstrued, misused, or abused. We fear that we'll end up on a no-fly list, or be unable to get a security clearance, a job, or a loan. We fear being wrongly accused, harassed, detained, and—in the era of targeted killings—who knows what else?

This points to an essential difference between the privacy of governments and the privacy of individuals: Governments have far more power than individuals. When the government's "privacy" is violated—through the unauthorized disclosure of classified documents, for instance—the government can prosecute the leakers, and it can generally fall back on multiple other means to preventing the harms it wants to prevent. The NSA's Internet and telephone data collection capabilities are not the U.S. government's sole means of preventing terrorist attacks, for instance: It has many other ways to gather intelligence and other ways to disrupt and defang terrorist organizations.

In contrast, individuals have far less power and far fewer ways to protect themselves. The cards are stacked in favor of the government. This is all the more true in the post-9/11 environment, in which the government has the advantage of permissive laws, deferential courts and congressmen, "black" budgets, and a vast national security bureaucracy that has expanded faster than our collective ability to control it.

I've made this point in a previous column, but I'll make it again here:

> The problem [with NSA surveillance practices] is not a privacy problem at all, but an accountability problem. . . . Given the current lack of transparency, we don't know what rules govern who can see what data, under what circumstances, for what purposes, and with what consequences. We don't know if this sweeping data collection has led to mistakes or abuses that have harmed innocent people, and we don't know what recourse an innocent person would have if harmed in some way.
>
> [T]here needs to be a mechanism to remedy [any] damage and impose appropriate consequences on government wrongdoers. If these data collection practices (or any similar past practices) lead to innocent people getting stuck on no-fly lists, or getting harassed by federal agents, or ending up wrongly detained, there should be a prompt, transparent, and fair means for them to challenge their treatment, see the supposed evidence against them, and get the problem fixed.

"Privacy" is a red herring in the debate about NSA surveillance (and many other kinds of covert activities). If we want meaningful reform, we need to set aside the rhetoric of privacy and focus instead on creating genuine safeguards against the abuse of government power.

> "All presumptions should favor the natural rights of individuals, not the delegated and seized powers of the government."

The Use of Surveillance Drones Is a Threat to Privacy

Andrew Napolitano

In the following viewpoint, Andrew Napolitano argues that drones will be used for government surveillance in the future and that Americans need to oppose this violation of individual liberty. Napolitano claims that a recent US government document wrongly privileges intelligence gathering over freedom. He contends that government assaults on privacy are equivalent to violence and must be opposed. Napolitano, a former judge of the Superior Court of New Jersey, is the senior judicial analyst at Fox News Channel.

As you read, consider the following questions:

1. Which American founder does Napolitano argue would have opposed the use of drones for surveillance?

2. According to the author, for what reason do we have the Constitution and life-tenured judiciary?

3. What is the reason Napolitano gives for why individual liberty, and not government power, is the default position?

For the past few weeks [May–June 2012], I have been writing in this column about the government's use of drones and challenging their constitutionality on Fox News Channel where I work. I once asked on air what Thomas Jefferson would have done if—had drones existed at the time—King George III had sent drones to peer inside the bedroom windows of Monticello. I suspect that Jefferson and his household would have trained their muskets on the drones and taken them down. I offer this historical anachronism as a hypothetical only, not as one who is urging the use of violence against the government.

The Future of Drones

Nevertheless, what Jeffersonians are among us today? When drones take pictures of us on our private property and in our homes, and the government uses the photos as it wishes, what will we do about it? Jefferson understood that when the government assaults our privacy and dignity, it is the moral equivalent of violence against us. The folks who hear about this, who either laugh or groan, cannot find it humorous or boring that their every move will be monitored and photographed by the government.

Don't believe me that this is coming? The photos that the drones will take may be retained and used or even distributed to others in the government so long as the "recipient is reasonably perceived to have a specific, lawful governmental function" in requiring them. And for the first time since the Civil War, the federal government will deploy military personnel *in-*

side the United States and publicly acknowledge that it is deploying them "to collect information about U.S. persons."

It gets worse. If the military personnel see something of interest from a drone, they may apply to a military judge or "military commander" for permission to conduct a physical search of the private property that intrigues them. And, any "incidentally acquired information" can be retained or turned over to local law enforcement. What's next? Prosecutions before military tribunals in the U.S.?

The quoted phrases above are extracted from a now-public 30-page memorandum issued by President [Barack] Obama's secretary of the Air Force on April 23, 2012. The purpose of the memorandum is stated as "balancing . . . obtaining intelligence information . . . and protecting individual rights guaranteed by the U.S. Constitution. . . ." Note the primacy of intelligence gathering over freedom protection, and note the peculiar use of the word "balancing."

A Bias in Favor of Liberty

When liberty and safety clash, do we really expect the government to balance those values? Of course not. The government cannot be trusted to restrain itself in the face of individual choices to pursue happiness. That's why we have a Constitution and a life-tenured judiciary: to protect the minority from the liberty-stealing impulses of the majority. And that's why the Air Force memo has its priorities reversed—intelligence gathering first, protecting freedom second—and the mechanism of reconciling the two—balancing them—constitutionally incorrect.

Everyone who works for the government swears to uphold the Constitution. It was written to define and restrain the government. According to the Declaration of Independence, the government's powers come from the consent of the governed. The government in America was not created by a powerful king reluctantly granting liberty to his subjects. It was created by free people willingly granting limited power to their government—and retaining that which they did not delegate.

The declaration also defines our liberties as coming from our Creator, as integral to our humanity and as inseparable from us, unless we give them up by violating someone else's liberties. Hence the Jeffersonian and constitutional beef with the word "balancing" when it comes to government power versus individual liberty.

The Judeo-Christian and constitutionally mandated relationship between government power and individual liberty is not balance. It is *bias*—a bias in favor of liberty. All presumptions should favor the natural rights of individuals, not the delegated and seized powers of the government. Individual liberty, not government power, is the default position because persons are immortal and created in God's image, and governments are temporary and based on force.

The Issue of Consent

Hence my outrage at the coming use of drones—some as small as golf balls—to watch us, to listen to us and to record us. Did you consent to the government having that power? Did you consent to the American military spying on Americans in America? I don't know a single person who has, but I know only a few who are complaining.

If we remain silent when our popularly elected government violates the laws it has sworn to uphold and steals the freedoms we elected it to protect, we will have only ourselves to blame when Big Brother is everywhere. Somehow, I doubt my father's generation fought the Nazis in World War II only to permit a totalitarian government to flourish here.

Is President Obama prepared to defend this? . . . Are you prepared for its consequences?

*"Without an overall legal framework
that aligns state laws, an overabundance of regulation has the potential to
ground the drone industry before it ever
takes off."*

Privacy Concerns Should
Not Stunt the Growth
of the Drone Industry

Pierre Hines

*In the following viewpoint, Pierre Hines argues that although
there are legitimate concerns about safety and privacy related to
the growth of the drone industry, there is a risk in enacting legislation that would limit the benefits of drone use. Hines contends that there are many valuable uses for drones beyond surveillance. A national legal framework, he concludes, could help
regulate for safety and privacy, while allowing the growth of the
industry for many uses. Hines is a Defense Council member of
the Truman National Security Project and a former US Army
intelligence officer.*

As you read, consider the following questions:

1. The author claims that the Federal Aviation Administration (FAA) estimates that there will be how many drones in US airspace within the next twenty years?

2. What has been the military's most frequent use for drones thus far, according to the author?

3. Hines claims that legislation to restrict drone use amid privacy concerns has been proposed in at least how many states?

Unmanned aerial vehicles (UAVs) are most commonly referred to as drones, but other names such as "killer robot" and "Big Brother in the sky" have surfaced. Regardless of what they're called, one thing is clear: Drones are here to stay and will increasingly be used for nonmilitary, domestic applications.

The Uses of Drones

The Federal Aviation Administration (FAA) estimates that there will be 30,000 drones in U.S. airspace within the next 20 years. The news of future drone proliferation has sparked controversy among many Americans who have legitimate safety and privacy concerns, but who narrowly view drones as either spying or overseas killing machines. Although legislative and regulatory oversight is warranted, an onslaught of incoherent drone regulation isn't, and it could cause setbacks in an industry that has the potential to usher in significant benefits to the economy and everyday lives of Americans.

As a former Army intelligence officer who frequently utilized drones, I originally shared the same narrow concerns about their dangers and potential menace. I mainly viewed them as counterterrorism and law enforcement tools that were used in one of two ways: for surveillance purposes or for lethal effects. However, it's clear that drones have other applications. Private parties have been authorized to use drones for experimental purposes, including some universities that are developing new methods of monitoring agriculture. Another use involves conducting missions that serve the public interest—e.g., search and rescue, border patrol, and firefighting missions. In fact, the National Aeronautics and Space Administration (NASA) has used drones to monitor hurricanes, and during the recent fire at Yosemite National Park in California, a drone was used to track the blaze's path.

It's currently illegal to fly drones over major urban areas or use them for commercial purposes, but if and when that changes, drones might be used for everyday tasks like transporting equipment, people, and possibly your online Amazon purchases.

The Issue of Safety

The first major obstacle to introducing drones for routine domestic use is concerns about the danger posed by malfunctions and crashes. The FAA already regulates the industry, like it does for commercial aircraft, and it manages safety risks by requiring drone operators to apply for certification. These certificates usually expire after two years and come with specific requirements like registering with air-traffic control, flying below a certain altitude, and flying only during daylight hours in some cases.

As of early 2013, there were more than 300 active Certificates of Waiver or Authorization. Next the FAA will establish six test sites across the country to conduct a full evaluation of how drones can be safely integrated into available airspace.

Still, it's inevitable that drones will crash; I've experienced it during military operations overseas, and it will happen when drones operate domestically. But piloted planes also crash and it hasn't led to them being categorically banned, and there is little evidence to suggest that drones are inherently more dangerous. After the test sites are established, the

The Uses of Drones

Safety inspectors used drones at Japan's crippled Fukushima Daiichi nuclear power plant to survey the damage after last year's [2011's] tsunami. Archaeologists in Russia are using small drones with infrared cameras to construct a 3-D model of ancient burial mounds. Environmental activists use the Osprey drone to track and monitor Japanese whaling ships. Photographers are developing a celebrity-seeking paparazzi drone. . . . Drones will soon fly into hurricanes to more accurately monitor a storm's strength.

Micah Zenko,
"10 Things You Didn't Know About Drones,"
Foreign Policy, *February 27, 2012.*

FAA and the drone industry will gain a deeper understanding of the issues that require additional safety precautions and implement further regulatory measures. Once those safety considerations are fleshed out, the FAA should move forward in integrating drones with as much risk mitigation as possible, while keeping in mind that eliminating *all* risk is impractical.

The Issue of Privacy

The second major obstacle to the proliferation of drones is the fear that they will infringe on individuals' privacy. These are valid concerns given recent revelations about the expansion of the state's surveillance reach and the ongoing growth in the private data-collection market, but they betray a misunderstanding about how drones operate. It's critical to understand that drones are not inherently surveillance tools, though that has been the military's most frequent use for them thus far. The technology itself is only about flying without pilots, not snooping from above. Other military technologies have been successfully adapted for domestic use without posing a significant threat to public safety or well-being, and drones should be no exception.

However, given the precedent for drone use, there is a legitimate fear that law enforcement officials will use them to monitor the activities of American citizens, a scenario made possible by advancements in "wide-area surveillance." Military drones, with ominous code names like Predator, can monitor movement across an entire urban area. Efforts to curtail the domestic use of drones generally call for four privacy protections: (1) limiting tracking operations to specific individuals; (2) obtaining a warrant; (3) discarding any data unrelated to the specific target of the investigation; and (4) denying the use of drone-collected evidence in court if the evidence was obtained unlawfully or unintentionally.

The current legal regime is well suited to deal with most, but not all, of the privacy concerns drones create. For instance, it is settled law that high-powered technology cannot be used without a warrant to spy on Americans in their residences because the home is a protected place under the Constitution. One issue the legal regime is not prepared for is how to deal with constant surveillance *outside* the home—in parks, on roads, and in other public areas. Theoretically, the police could still tail you to accomplish the same objective without a warrant, but limited resources serve as a check on this power. The decreasing cost of drones and increasing capabilities mean that drones won't strain police resources the same way old-fashioned police work would.

The Need for a Legal Framework

Legislation to restrict drone use amid privacy concerns has been proposed in at least 42 states. That isn't the problem; the problem is that there's no coherent legal framework at a national level. One of the many benefits of drones is the ability to travel long distances, but if the law changes every time a drone crosses a county line, it could significantly affect the cost-benefit analysis of using them.

While safety and privacy concerns are well founded, we shouldn't let them stunt the growth of an entire industry. And without an overall legal framework that aligns state laws, an overabundance of regulation has the potential to ground the drone industry before it ever takes off. Beyond the military and law enforcement applications, drones have the potential to benefit our lives in everything from disaster relief to assessing power lines. In the not-too-distant future, if drone policy is properly established, you might look up and see not a bird, not a plane, but a drone.

| *"Biometrics are the future of identification, and the future is almost here."*

Biometrics Are the Future of Identification

Tim De Chant

In the following viewpoint, Tim De Chant argues that in the future, biometric data—such as fingerprints, voice analysis, and iris patterns—will be used for identification. De Chant contends that societies have always needed to identify individuals and that biometrics can fulfil that need with greater security. De Chant notes that there are privacy concerns with the use of biometrics and issues of information security that will need to be addressed for the technology to move forward. De Chant is the senior digital editor at NOVA and editor of the NOVA Next website.

As you read, consider the following questions:

1. The author cites an anthropologist who claims that human beings can recognize, or identify, an average of how many faces?

2. What country has the largest biometric identification system, according to the author?

3. What example does the author give of a current use of identification that gives a glimpse into the future of biometrics in the world of commerce?

It's a dreary March morning in Massachusetts, and I'm sitting in my car in an anonymous office park an hour outside of Boston trying to understand what just happened. I'm here because I wanted to get a better grasp on biometric identification, specifically what it's like for a person like you or me, who hasn't committed a crime but, at some point in the near future, will use some part of our bodies to confirm a credit card purchase or enter a foreign country. I'm trying to square what just took place inside with what I had secretly hoped would happen.

The Use of Biometrics

Biometric identification has a faint whiff of the future about it, though what that future looks like depends entirely on your perspective. It could be a dystopian world, often seen in movies, novels, and comic books where Big Brother haunts our heroes, monitoring them through iris scans or facial recognition. Or it could be a sleek and polished future, where speaking an authorization code grants you control of a vehicle or glancing at a camera opens a locked door with a hushed hiss.

But what I had just experienced was neither. Inside at Aware Inc., a Bedford, Mass., company that makes software for biometric systems, Sarah Fischer, a programmer, had walked me through the process of scanning my fingerprints. She had me place my right fingers on the scanner, then my left, then both thumbs. The software would let her know if my prints were successfully captured.

I failed at first, if you can fail at such a thing. Press harder, Sarah had said. That seemed to do the trick, but my second attempt still took longer than it should have—38 seconds to scan all ten fingerprints. According to guidelines issued by the federal government, the process should take 20 seconds or less.

Despite the hiccup, my first experience with biometrics was neither flashy nor frightening. In fact, it was kind of boring (no offense to Sarah), which is actually kind of exciting—biometrics are sufficiently advanced to be almost unremarkable. Just in time, too. Soon, our smartphones and tablets will employ some form of biometric identification to keep our personal data private. Before long, physical driver's licenses will be obsolete and credit card purchases won't require signatures, just a wave of our hands over a sensor. And it won't take dozens of seconds like my fingerprinting, but one or two.

As I pull out of Aware's nondescript parking lot, I'm starting to believe what all those scientists and researchers have been telling me these past few weeks. Biometrics are the future of identification, and the future is almost here.

A Need to ID

Since the earliest days of human history, we've needed to verify who the people around us are. In more recent times, as the human population has surged into the billions, that need has only intensified. Are you part of the tribe, or are you an outsider? According to research by Robin Dunbar, an anthropologist at Oxford University, the average person can only recognize about 1,500 faces. That's a pretty astonishing number, but it pales in comparison to the numbers of people we come into contact with over a month or even a day.

Today, our identities are verified almost exclusively by one of two methods—things that you carry with you and things you remember. Driver's licenses and passports are examples of the former, passwords and PINs the latter. But physical identification is easy to fake, and passwords are easily cracked by hackers, who then have nearly unfettered access to our credit cards, bank accounts, and personal data. Something needs to change.

Biometrics could be that change. They are a fundamental shift in the way we are identified. Unlike traditional identification which you must either remember or carry with you, biometrics *are* you. Fingerprints, voice analysis, iris patterns, vein matching, gait analysis, and so on. Such traits are unique to an individual and often, though not always, incredibly difficult to fake.

Some concepts behind biometrics are old, dating back to the late 1800s. Sir William Herschel, a British magistrate in India, looked into fingerprints as a unique identifier for individuals, and later Sir Francis Galton, Charles Darwin's cousin, developed a method for classifying fingerprints. The technology was quickly applied to criminal investigations, and to this day, suspects around the world are fingerprinted after their arrest.

For more than 100 years, that was about the extent of it. It wasn't until the 1990s that computers and scanners had become sufficiently advanced to support true biometric identification. But even then, their use was limited primarily to law enforcement.

The Watershed Moment

Then 9/11 [referring to the September 11, 2001, terrorist attacks on the United States] happened. Suddenly, the U.S. government became acutely aware that it didn't know exactly who was passing in and out of the country. "After 9/11, the U.S. Congress decided we must have some way of securing our borders," says Anil Jain, a computer scientist at [Michigan State] University. The terrorist attack, he says, was a "major watershed."

The use of biometrics has spread rapidly. "In the past 12 years since 9/11, the amount of biometrics collected in the

United States has increased exponentially," says Jennifer Lynch, an attorney with the Electronic Frontier Foundation.

That's in part because the U.S. government has poured money into research, development, and acquisition of biometric identification systems. The Department of Homeland Security has spent over $133 million on biometrics since 2003 and the Defense Department is predicted to spend $3.5 billion on the technology between 2007–2015. The FBI [Federal Bureau of Investigation] has rapidly expanded its fingerprint database and is currently developing a more sophisticated system that will add iris scans, palm scans, and facial recognition to the mix. The U.S. Department of Homeland Security has its own system called US-VISIT [United States Visitor and Immigrant Status Indicator Technology], for which non-U.S. passport holders are required to submit all 10 fingerprints and a digital photograph before leaving for the U.S. When they enter the country, their biometrics are collected again and compared against a database of many possible matches to verify their identity.

The U.S. military, too, uses biometrics extensively. Its first widespread applications were in Iraq and Afghanistan. In an attempt to weed out insurgents from the general public, the U.S. military has collected fingerprints, iris scans, and facial images from millions of Iraqis and Afghans.

Other countries are rolling out biometric identification systems for their own citizens. India's is the largest to date. Introduced in 2010, it has over 200 million people currently enrolled. Unlike many other biometric databases, which are aimed at finding criminals, India's system will eventually encompass everyone in the country. India's millions of poor often lack official identification, complicating the allocation of aid and other social services. Biometrics will serve as a form of national ID that can't be lost or misplaced.

The Concerns About Privacy

But just because they can't be lost or misplaced doesn't mean they can't be misused. Privacy concerns loom large with biometrics. A biometric by itself isn't threatening, though they are easily linked to other, potentially sensitive information, and that's when people grow uneasy.

Some of the anxiety stems from the fact that biometrics are a part of who we are—they're not an Internet username that can be easily discarded or created anew. Biometrics will likely persist in government and private databases, accreting information whether we like it or not.

"I think the biggest problem with biometric collection is that once the government has your biometric, it becomes incredibly useful for a whole host of purposes, and the government tends not to want to delete it," Lynch says. Until recently, the only people who were fingerprinted were criminals or those who had to undergo background checks. But with biometrics, more people are likely to be caught in the net, and the consequences could be wide-ranging. "We've seen that with some of the data-sharing programs in the federal government right now," Lynch says. "A biometric collected for an immigration purpose could then be used for a criminal purpose."

The debate over the extent and uses of government databases has intensified since the public became aware of the surveillance program PRISM, run by the National Security Agency, known as the NSA. According to news reports citing leaked confidential information, the NSA created PRISM to monitor the electronic communications and digital bread crumbs of foreigners suspected of being terrorists. It siphons data about phone calls, search histories, e-mail messages, and more from private servers run by technology companies, including Google, Facebook, and others. The volume is so great that innocent U.S. citizens are likely caught in the broad net.

The Use of Personal Biometrics

While biometrics haven't been mentioned as being stored in the PRISM database, there's a good chance a biometric of yours is stored in at least one of those companies' databases—Facebook. "Facebook has the largest facial recognition database in the entire world," Lynch says. Whenever someone uploads a photo to Facebook, the company's algorithms scan the image for faces and sifts through their own records to suggest a name. It sounds innocuous enough, but there's no guarantee they won't be used for another purpose in the future.

"When you're dealing with a private company, where your interaction with that company is governed by a term of use, the company could change it at any time," Lynch says. [Researcher Marios] Savvides shares those concerns, too. It seems increasingly unlikely that people will be able to control who or what has access to their personal information, including biometrics. "I don't think that it's easy to exist in today's society without using these services," Lynch says. "We all make phone calls, we all send e-mails, most of us use Facebook, a lot of us use Apple products. I think it's a false choice to say that we have any kind of choice over sharing our data with third parties."

That doesn't sit well with Senator Al Franken. "I think that people have a fundamental right to privacy," he tells me. "We have the right to tell people exactly where we are and what we're doing or to remain anonymous in a crowd. I'm concerned with the potential uses of facial recognition technology because this technology makes it exceedingly easy to infringe that right."

"This technology is already in wide deployment by commercial entities like Facebook and state governments, and federal law enforcement," Franken says. "I'm worried that we're rolling this technology out without adequately considering its consequences or putting the right protections in place."

Franken has been the most vocal elected official pushing for regulation of biometrics, but unfortunately his efforts have stalled. "Last summer, Senator Franken was looking into facial recognition limitations, and we haven't seen anything with that," Lynch says. The problem, she says, is a familiar one: "Congress is inherently gridlocked."

The Protection of Biometrics

While current regulations lag behind technology, researchers are feverishly working to address people's concerns—namely, what happens if a database holding your biometrics gets hacked? You can reset a password, but you can't replace your fingertips or eyeballs. To work around this problem, computer scientists have been exploring two promising ways to link individuals with their fingerprints, iris scans, and other features without exposing the original biometric to hackers, even if the system is compromised.

One approach is to store biometric data in what's called a hash. Hashes are widely used in computing as a way of encoding data that masks information about the original. They are commonly used to store passwords in databases. Each hashed password is unique, and changing just one character in a password produces a hash that's completely different. Depending on the hashing function, decoding a hash can be extremely time-consuming. You can cryptographically hash any digital file, including images of fingerprints and other biometrics. Hashes are relatively secure because they are computed using one-way functions, which means they are computationally easy in one direction (encrypting) but hard in the other (decrypting).

Since we already hash passwords, it seems logical that we'd also hash biometrics. Unfortunately, it's not as straightforward. That's because passwords can be reliably entered the same way every time, but no two biometric scans are identical, says Shantanu Rane, a research scientist at the Mitsubishi

Electric Research Laboratories in Cambridge, Mass. Hashing the resulting images would produce wildly different results, making matching impossible without inverting the hash, which would take an unreasonably long time. To sidestep this problem, researchers first extract features that can be reliably reproduced most of the time but don't reveal the underlying biometric. For fingerprints, these would include collections of points such as ridge ends or bifurcations. These features are encoded and then stored in a database. The original images are never stored in the system. If the system is hacked, these encodings are thrown out and new ones are issued.

There is still a chance that hackers could eventually reverse the stored encodings, though. At that point, they would have access to the original biometrics, which would compromise both security and privacy. A better way would be to encrypt a biometric prior to storage and never decrypt it. But if you never decrypt the original, how do you compare it to a submitted biometric? The answer, Rane says, is to perform all computations required for the comparison in the encrypted domain. That way, even if a hacker is snooping on the system, they'll never see unencrypted data. Everything on the computer is encrypted. The downside is that while theoretically possible, such computations are incredibly complex today. "There is a lot of research happening today on computation in the encrypted domain," Rane says. He predicts that we might see such computers in the near future.

Encoding and computing in the encrypted domain could go a long way to securing databases. But there are other uses for biometrics that wouldn't put any personal information at risk. In fact, it's possible that the broadest use of biometrics—completing purchases—won't require that they be stored on centralized databases.

Known as verification, the technique simply compares a submitted biometric with a reference copy stored on a device like a credit card, which is carried by its owner, Jain says. To use it, you would insert your card into a reader and then present your biometric. The reader would compare your submitted biometric with the record on the card. If the two match, the transaction would be approved. It's just like the signature on the back of your credit card, but less easily faked. Plus, Jain points out, "There is no centralized place where your fingerprint is stored."

Real-World Uses of Biometrics

Already, we're seeing glimpses of what this biometric future will look like. Electronic payment company Square recently released a feature where you can pay simply by carrying your phone in your pocket or purse. When you walk in a shop, Square's software will bring up your photo on the store's register. If you want to buy something, a clerk can complete the transaction by verifying that the image on the screen is, in fact, you. It's a similar process to that used at border crossings in many countries, where citizens or visitors wave their electronic passports over a sensor and immigration officials verify that the information stored on the passport matches the individual in front of them.

With these systems, Savvides says, "the human is doing the biometric matching." They aren't fully automated, which means they fall short of what researchers like Savvides consider true biometric systems. But they're "starting to bridge the gap," he says. It's easy to imagine replacing the human in these situations with a camera and a computer. "Wouldn't it just be so much faster and increase throughput to have an automated system that does that?" he asks.

That may happen someday soon, but we're not quite there yet. A few weeks ago, I had my first real-life experience with biometrics. I had just gotten off a 14.5 hour flight from New York to Tokyo when I stepped up to an immigration officer, who instructed me to look into the camera and place my fingers on the scanner. Bleary-eyed, I stared into a pinhole above the monitor and then rested my fingertips on a green-glowing plate. I waited for an affirmative that didn't come. The officer mumbled something I couldn't hear.

"I'm sorry?" I asked him.

"Press harder."

"The reliability of the technology is only one aspect of the different problems around governments' collection of biometrics, including privacy, security, profiling, discrimination, and other civil liberties."

Biometric Identification Raises Privacy Concerns Without Increasing Security

Katitza Rodriguez

In the following viewpoint, Katitza Rodriguez argues that the use of biometric technologies with national identification and passports gives a false sense of security, as such technologies have many problems with accuracy and in preventing fraud. Given the problems with privacy, discrimination, and other concerns, Rodriguez claims that governments have not succeeded in making a successful argument for the use of biometric identification. Rodriguez is the international rights director for the Electronic Frontier Foundation.

As you read, consider the following questions:

1. According to Rodriguez, biometric data of individuals' faces has been used since what year at various European border checks?

2. European Union law requires what biometric data for passports in countries in the Schengen area, according to the author?

3. The author claims that a report in France found that what percentage of biometric passports were fraudulently obtained?

People tend to think that digital copies of our biological features, stored in a government-run database, are problems of a dystopian future. But governments around the world are already using such technologies. Several countries are collecting massive amounts of biometric data for their national identity and passport schemes—a development that raises significant civil liberties and privacy concerns. Biometric identifiers are inherently sensitive data. As European privacy watchdogs have said, biometrics change irrevocably the relationship between body and identity, because they make the characteristics of the human body "machine-readable" and subject to further use. This is why such identification schemes become particularly dangerous when used with unreliable biometric technologies that can misidentify individuals.

The Use of Biometric Technologies

Regulators in several jurisdictions continue to romanticize the security and accuracy of face, fingerprint, and iris automatic recognition biometric technologies. But the existence of a significant amount of falsified biometric identification documents raises questions as to whether these technologies are too unreliable to prevent fraud, thus providing individuals and governments with a false sense of security.

Biometric data of individuals' faces have been used since 2007 at various European border checks. Eleven airports in the United Kingdom [UK] now have e-passport gates that scan EU [European Union] travelers' faces and compare them to measurements of their facial features (i.e., biometrics), stored on a chip in their biometric passports. Although error rates of state-of-the-art facial recognition technologies have been reduced over the past 20 years, these technologies still cannot identify individuals with complete accuracy. In an incident in 2011, the Manchester e-passport gates let through a couple that had mixed up their passports. The UK Border Agency subsequently disabled the Manchester gates and launched an investigation.

Similar e-passport gates have been introduced in Australia and New Zealand. During the early stages of testing in Australia, the technology showed a six to eight percent error rate. Moreover, this technology also misidentified two men who exchanged passports. Nevertheless, the government refused to disclose the final error rates, citing security concerns.

The Use of Digital Fingerprint Recognition

U.S. law requires visitors to submit biometrics to a central database in the form of a digital fingerprint when seeking a visa or when entering the country. EU law further requires all passports for 26 countries in the Schengen area (the borderless zone within European countries) to contain digital fingerprint data on a chip.

The United Kingdom—a non-Schengen country—contemplated introducing fingerprints voluntarily as part of a biometric passport 2.0, but ultimately decided against it. The UK government was preparing to launch a biometric national identity card, for which it gathered fingerprints from 15,000 volunteers for the project. But the new government "didn't believe ID cards would work" and physically destroyed the pilot identity databases. However, in 2010, the UK National Policing Improvement Agency also conducted a pilot test to provide police officers with digital fingerprint scanners that could remotely match individuals' fingerprints against a central database. The outcome of this project is unknown and, when questioned, the agency refused to disclose the error rates that resulted from its tests.

In the Netherlands, the database storage of digital fingerprinting for travel documents was halted following questions over the reliability of the biometric technology. The mayor of the city of Roermond reported that 21 percent of fingerprints collected in the city could not be used to identify any individuals. In April 2011, the Dutch minister of the interior, in a letter to the Dutch House of Representatives, asserted that the number of false rejections (cases in which there is a "no-hit" for a lawful holder of a travel document) is too high to warrant using fingerprints for verification and identification. Currently, only fingerprints onto radio-frequency identification (RFID) chips in ID documents are being collected.

A German court recently asked the EU Court of Justice for a preliminary ruling on the legality of biometric passports with RFID chips, which are readable from a distance. The German court questioned whether the EU regulation that requires biometric passports in Europe is compatible with Charter of Fundamental Rights of the European Union and the European Convention on Human Rights.

In France, a report last year [2011] disclosed the questionable security of biometric passports. It showed that 10 percent of biometric passports were fraudulently obtained for illegal immigrants or people looking for a new identity. Following the issues with respect to biometric passports in the various EU countries, members of the European Parliament have queried the European Commission about the reliability of these biometric passports.

The Use of Iris Scan Identification

In preparation for the UK's national ID card scheme, the UK government noted that there was little research indicating the reliability of iris scan identification. The government initially relied upon unpublished and unverified results from an airport trial. There were concerns that "hard contact lenses," "watery eyes and long eyelashes" could prevent accurate scanning. The government then asked the National Physical Laboratory (NPL) to test the technology. The NPL chief research scientist stated in the news that "technologies like iris scanning are accurate enough for the ID cards application but only provided they are implemented properly and one has appropriate fallback processes to deal with exceptional cases." But a study has shown that it is difficult to enroll disabled individuals into an iris database. The success of enrollment also significantly varies depending on race and age, suggesting further errors if the technology were implemented. Additional testing of iris scanners has been initiated by the U.S. Department of Homeland Security.

In summary, governments have failed to support their claim that such technologies actually improve security. These governments have not proved that the technology is reliable enough to prevent fraud. Of course, the reliability of the technology is only one aspect of the different problems around governments' collection of biometrics, including privacy, security, profiling, discrimination, and other civil liberties.

Periodical and Internet Sources Bibliography

The following articles have been selected to supplement the diverse views presented in this chapter.

Brad Allenby	"The Golden Age of Privacy Is Over, but Drones Aren't to Blame," *Slate*, April 30, 2013.
Julia Angwin	"U.S. Terrorism Agency to Tap a Vast Database of Citizens," *Wall Street Journal*, December 13, 2012.
David Bier	"The New National Identification System Is Coming," Competitive Enterprise Institute, February 1, 2013.
Zoë Carpenter	"The Internet Giants Oppose Surveillance—but Only When the Government Does It," *Nation*, December 16, 2013.
Conor Friedersdorf	"The Dangerous, False Trade-Off Between Liberty and Security," *Atlantic*, August 23, 2012.
Glenn Greenwald	"Domestic Drones and Their Unique Dangers," *Guardian* (UK), March 29, 2013.
Robin Koerner	"Privacy vs. Security: A False Dichotomy," *Huffington Post*, April 5, 2014.
Steven Levy	"How the NSA Almost Killed the Internet," *Wired*, January 7, 2014.
Sara Sorcher	"The Backlash Against Drones," *National Journal*, February 21, 2013.
Eric Sterner	"The Security vs. Privacy Debate Is Already Over, and Privacy Lost," *Washington Examiner*, March 10, 2014.
Bruce Stokes	"Trading Privacy for Security," *Foreign Policy*, November 4, 2013.

OPPOSING
VIEWPOINTS®
SERIES

CHAPTER 3

Is Medical Privacy Adequately Protected?

Chapter Preface

The Health Insurance Portability and Accountability Act of 1996 (HIPAA) was passed, in part, to address issues of privacy related to health care and medical records. The first part of the act, Title I, allows people to keep health insurance coverage if they lose a job or take a new job. The second part, Title II, provides privacy and security standards for doctors, hospitals, and insurers in handling patient health information. Nonetheless, many argue that medical privacy is not adequately protected by this act or any other existing legislation.

The HIPAA Privacy Rule regulates the use and disclosure of protected health information, or PHI. To protect patients' medical privacy, the rule requires that any disclosure of PHI beyond that required by law enforcement or administrative purposes needs written authorization from the patient for disclosure. The rule also allows patients to correct inaccurate PHI and requires health care entities to notify patients of uses of their PHI.

Beginning in April 2003, when compliance with the HIPAA Privacy Rule became required, the Office for Civil Rights (OCR) began accepting complaints involving the privacy of personal health information in the health care system. The US Department of Health and Human Services and OCR reported in April 2014 that they had received more than 95,588 HIPAA complaints and that more than 90,411 had been resolved. They additionally reported that more than 22,497 cases were investigated and resolved by requiring corrective actions on the part of the health care entities investigated. In 10,114 cases, no violation of HIPAA was found, and 57,800 cases were lacking eligibility for enforcement. The OCR reports that the five most common compliance issues investigated were:

1. Impermissible uses and disclosures of protected health information;

2. Lack of safeguards of protected health information;

3. Lack of patient access to their protected health information;

4. Uses or disclosures of more than the minimum necessary standard of protected health information; and

5. Lack of administrative safeguards of electronic protected health information.

Many critics say that HIPAA does not go far enough in protecting privacy. The Electronic Frontier Foundation (EFF) contends that HIPAA "is severely limited because it only applies to an entity if it is what the law considers to be either a 'covered entity'—namely: a health care provider, health plan, or health care clearinghouse." EFF is also concerned that there are too many exceptions to when health care information may be disclosed without consent, such as for national security purposes.

As the authors in this chapter illustrate, there are numerous concerns about the privacy of medical information. Even among those who agree that individuals ought to have control over private health care information, much disagreement exists about how to go about safeguarding that information without sacrificing health care quality.

> "A private corporation, backed by some of the largest tech companies in the world (including Google), is planning to do genetic research through statistical modeling on an unprecedented scale."

Private DNA Tests Raise a Variety of Privacy Concerns

Benjamin Winterhalter

In the following viewpoint, Benjamin Winterhalter argues that the rise in direct-to-consumer DNA tests is raising questions about how the storage of genetic information is going to be regulated. Winterhalter contends that although the current planned use of stored genetic information is for medical purposes, there is no reason to think the use of such information will remain in that realm. He worries that the current intention to safeguard the privacy of genetic information may not remain if other uses are developed. Winterhalter is an attorney in Massachusetts.

Benjamin Winterhalter, "A Genetic 'Minority Report': How Corporate DNA Testing Could Put Us at Risk," *Salon*, January 26, 2014. This article first appeared in Salon.com, at http://www.Salon.com. An online version remains in the Salon archives. Reprinted with permission.

As you read, consider the following questions:

1. According to the author, how many individuals have sent genetic information to the testing company 23andMe?

2. The author contends that the recent US Supreme Court decision in *Maryland v. King* ruled that what police action is constitutional?

3. Why does the author think it is unlikely that a genetic privacy law will get passed?

On Nov. 22, 2013, the FDA [US Food and Drug Administration] sent a now-infamous letter to the genetic research start-up 23andMe, ordering the company to stop marketing some of its personal DNA testing kits. In its letter, the agency told 23andMe that it was concerned about the possibility of erroneous test results, about false positives and false negatives. The FDA warned that false positives—for example, being told that one has a high risk of breast cancer when really one doesn't—might lead customers to seek expensive testing or medical treatment that they don't really need. False negatives—which are just the opposite—might lead customers to ignore serious health problems or deviate from a prescribed treatment regimen. The company had been out of contact with the FDA since May of 2013, and had not filed the required information to allay the bureau's concerns.

The Legal Perspective

When word about the letter got out, the ever-ready machine of Internet journalism whirred quickly to life. Defenders of the genetic research firm argued that the information, if used properly and with a physician's supervision, is not only a wondrous tool for protecting health and prolonging life, but a fascinating look into the mysteries of one's genetic code. Besides, they continued, the technology is here to stay; fighting it will be like lashing the sea to stop the tide. Critics, however, shared the FDA's worries that the company's products might drive a frenzy of self-diagnosis and hypochondria. In their view, putting unfiltered diagnostic information in an anxiety-prone person's hands could be dangerous—better to leave it to the trained judgment of a licensed doctor. Neurologists have reported, for example, that otherwise healthy twenty-somethings, upon getting back their 23andMe results, have marched into their clinics demanding MRIs to check for signs of Alzheimer's [disease].

But how does 23andMe's process actually work? Upon receiving a saliva sample from a customer, 23andMe draws statistical inferences about that person's likelihood of having certain diseases based on what are called "single nucleotide polymorphisms" or "SNPs" (pronounced "snips"). A SNP is a genetic mutation at a single, specific location along a person's DNA strand. Rather than the base pair that the vast majority of the population has for a given location, an individual with a SNP has a different base pair, which can lead to anomalies in the production of amino acids (i.e., proteins in the body). When 23andMe finds certain SNPs in someone's DNA, it then cross-references its vast databases of medical literature, which contain findings from thousands of studies showing correlations between certain SNPs and certain diseases. To guard against misinforming its customers, 23andMe maintains precise standards about which studies make it into its databases. The political fight about the company, thus, is drawing the troops into a swamp—into the muddy marsh of arguing over whether consumers are intelligent enough to process this sort of sophisticated statistical and epidemiological information on their own. The question quickly becomes not about 23andMe's little kits, but about government paternalism more generally.

Legally speaking, however, the entire argument is moot. There is no need to wade into the muck of one's feelings about big-government paternalism or the perils of new technologies—at least not right now. And that is for a simple reason: The FDA is right. According to the law, 23andMe's kit is a "medical device," which federal law defines as any product useful in diagnosis or treatment, which means that the kit is subject to the FDA's regulations about the marketing of medical products. Those regulations require 23andMe to provide the FDA with information about its statistical methods, to conduct studies of its products' effects, and to address the agency's concerns about the risks of erroneous test results. It hasn't done so. In the real world, thus, 23andMe *will* have to comply with the FDA's guidelines, and it *will* have to find some way of reassuring the government that its brightly colored little kit is not actually Pandora's box. From a legal perspective, that is the end of the discussion.

The Issue of Genetic Information

Which is not, of course, to say that it should end the discussion. There is another aspect of 23andMe's business, one which has received less attention from the media (with the exception of an excellent write-up in *Scientific American* by Charles Seife), but which is, in actuality, both equally troubling and equally fascinating. The company also houses a sizable research wing. 23andMe intends to aggregate the genetic information it receives and correlate that information with self-supplied data from customers about their biological traits— for instance, whether they clasp their hands with left thumb over right or vice versa; whether black coffee tastes bitter to them; or, more seriously, whether they have Parkinson's disease. According to its website, the company hopes to use this information to find new ways to predict the incidence of disease in the population.

If the project is successful, 23andMe's roof would shelter a veritable warehouse of genetic information, mapping correlations between phenotypes, SNPs and diseases across a huge swath of the population (albeit not a particularly diverse swath, given the company's likely market demographics). To date, 23andMe says that it has received saliva samples from approximately 500,000 people—a figure many times the size of those employed in most large-scale genetic studies—and the company has only existed since 2006. Once it clears its name with the FDA, the amount of genetic information available to the firm's research arm will only grow. "The long game here is not to make money selling kits, although the kits are essential to get the base-level data," said Patrick Chung, a 23andMe board member. And the company's privacy policy, it's worth noting, makes no promises that it will not share aggregate-level genetic data with its vendors and affiliates, such as the company that manufactures the chips used in processing saliva samples.

In a dashed-off write-up, Ezra Klein blithely opined that the company's research wing is simply "an experiment in big-data genetics." Citing Harvard political science professor Daniel Carpenter, who recently published a lengthy history of the FDA, Klein argued that new technologies like 23andMe's might provide a salubrious occasion to reevaluate how the law deals with cutting-edge bioinformatics. (How exactly the rules should change, though, Klein shrewdly declined to say.) There might be something to the point, but saying that we might possibly want to eventually give some consideration to maybe letting the political process (in consultation with appropriate experts, of course) arrive at some new rules about how such products might or might not be regulated is, ultimately, not to say much at all. It is almost as if Klein sees that there is a steep cliff off which he might take a sharp plunge into a sea of difficult and frightening questions, and decides instead simply to gesture offhandedly in its general direction.

But the only way forward is downward. Whatever happens to 23andMe, the *idea* of aggregating and cross-referencing huge amounts of genetic information is now a cultural reality. A private corporation, backed by some of the largest tech companies in the world (including Google), is planning to do genetic research through statistical modeling on an unprecedented scale. The implications of such a venture are profound, but the national conversation about the company has focused almost exclusively on what consumers will do with the information. This is not to say that it is not perfectly *reasonable* to have such a conversation. In fact, it is even reasonable to slosh around in the muddy waters of the swamp—the battle over paternalism and the authority of the medical establishment. But if we dare not ask, for example, whether an advanced, large-scale statistical model of human genetics might not be used to make predictions about, say, criminal behavior, or academic success, or lifetime income, who will? Let us dare to dive into the sea.

The Potential Uses of Genetic Information

To be clear, at present, 23andMe's databases are used for properly epidemiological purposes. And the company seems to be quite serious about protecting the privacy of customer data and fostering trust. Identifying information, for example, is encrypted and stored separately from genetic material. I am not, that is, accusing them of wrongdoing—of conspiring to create a genetic dystopia like the ones envisioned in films like *Gattaca* and *Minority Report*. Rather, I am suggesting that the *idea* of a massive genetic database holds all the ominous potential, if not used with extreme circumspection, to lead exactly there.

For instance, there is no reason, in principle, why the information available to 23andMe could not be used to make predictions about future crimes. With the information in 23andMe's hands, it would be possible, for example, to see whether you have the so-called warrior gene, the presence of which, a famous study found, correlates with a high likelihood of violent behavior, and then send you a "How likely are you to become a murderer?" report. There is also no reason why the company's statistical techniques could not be used to make predictions about intelligence. For example, the journal *Nature* reported last May [in 2013] that the Beijing Genomics Institute intends to study 1,600 mathematically and verbally gifted children (as measured by IQ) in a search for SNPs that might explain their extraordinary intelligence. If studies like this disclose significant results, and if their methods meet 23andMe's guidelines for scientific integrity, the company could begin marketing an all-new kit called "Will your baby become a super genius?"

From there, it is not hard to imagine going even further. Earlier this year, in *Maryland v. King*, the Supreme Court held, in a 5–4 ruling, that it was constitutional for the police to collect a sample of a person's DNA when he or she is arrested for—not even formally charged with—a crime. In a decision that none other than Justice [Antonin] Scalia criticized, in a fiery dissent, as authorizing the creation of a "genetic Panopticon," the court concluded that it was constitutional for the police to compare these DNA samples with national databases of DNA evidence found at the scenes of unsolved crimes. What is to stop the police from going further—from working together with bioinformatics companies like 23andMe to build a crime-prediction and crime-detection mega-model? Although 23andMe's information is currently stored in a form that makes it difficult for law enforcement to access, it would be possible in principle to cross-reference all three sources of information—bioinformatics customers, criminal arrestees and crime-scene evidence. With such a tool, the police could both find criminals foolish enough to want to know about their risks of disease and, more frighteningly, find SNPs that are correlated with getting arrested or committing crimes. Are we supposed to take comfort in the company's own privacy policy, which explicitly provides that it will surrender individual-level genetic material if required to do so by law? *Minority Report* indeed.

To many readers, worrying about these uses—and about whether they will lead to some sort of *Gattaca*-like dystopia— might sound like hyperbole, if not the ravings of a paranoid lunatic. After all, 23andMe has announced no plans to create such products. Asked for comment about these uses, 23andMe's Catherine Afarian quite reasonably told me that they are, at this point, "more science fiction than science fact." Furthermore, in 2008, Congress passed, with enormous bipartisan support and the signature of President George W. Bush, the Genetic Information Nondiscrimination Act or "GINA." GINA prohibits the use of information about a person's genetic predispositions in pricing health insurance or making employment decisions, such as hiring and promotion. So what, one might reasonably ask, is the problem? Isn't the only remaining question, indeed, the one about whether we think people are smart enough to process this sort of genetic information on their own?

But the point, again, is not only about *this particular company*, but about the broader trend toward making predictions about what will happen to someone based on the mutations in his or her genes. 23andMe is just the beginning; their kit is merely the prototype for a kind of bioinformatics product that companies will package and market to us in the years to come. They have, in fact, just proved that we are eager to buy. And while the passage of GINA undoubtedly represents a reassuring and admirable step toward ensuring that discoveries about our genetic predispositions are not used against us (though even then only in specific contexts), it cannot stop the momentum of our broader culture. Curiosity is a rushing river. If people want to know, the law cannot stop them from finding out. The only law that reigns when you click the button and send 23andMe your $99, when you follow the instructions and gather your saliva, when you then raptly read— with intense and morbid curiosity—the report that the company sends back, is the law of the market. At the end of the day, there is only you and the choices you make.

The Real Issue with Genetic Data

While the FDA [US Food and Drug Administration] concentrates on the question of whether 23andMe's kit is a safe and effective medical device, it is failing to address the real issue: what 23andMe should be allowed to do with the data it collects. . . . 23andMe's Personal Genome Service is much more than a medical device; it is a one-way portal into a world where corporations have access to the innermost contents of your cells and where insurers and pharmaceutical firms and marketers might know more about your body than you know yourself.

Charles Seife,
"23andMe Is Terrifying,
but Not for the Reasons the FDA Thinks,"
Scientific American, *November 27, 2013.*

The Possible Responses

What, then, are we supposed to do? There is at least one serious response available. We might, that is, not give up on the idea that we can reverse the tide. We have the power, if we choose to exercise it, to pass laws that would serve as significant bulwarks against the more insidious uses to which genetic data could be put. For example, we might still make laws to prohibit the police practices that the Supreme Court said were constitutional in *Maryland v. King.* Or we might pass a broader, more robust genetic nondiscrimination act, one that would bar the use of genetic information in education, in police profiling, in commerce and countless other arenas in which we otherwise enjoy civil rights. Or we might even pass a genetic privacy law, one that would outlaw certain data-sharing and retention practices and impose heavy penalties for violations. (This last option seems particularly far-fetched in a world where we apparently tolerate widespread spying by our own government.)

But I doubt that anything like this will happen. As it stands today, even if the FDA—the agency we all, in practice, must rely on to ensure the safety and integrity of these kinds of products—makes some new rules, 23andMe's kits, adorned with new warnings and restrictions, can return to market. And even if you, personally, decide not to participate in 23andMe's process, there is nothing you can do to stop others from placing an order for a kit. It appears that all we can do is hope. Maybe, if they are scrupulous, 23andMe will do nothing more than make contributions to epidemiology and to our understanding of our biological makeup. After all, there *are* millions of people in the world suffering with serious diseases, many of which likely have genetic links. Surely we should not wish to stop the gathering of data that could lead to major scientific breakthroughs?

Indeed not. It is, however, the good name of science that is treated most roughly in the national conversation about 23andMe. Many working scientists (ironically including some at 23andMe) maintain a ferocious skepticism about the power of correlational genetic studies to reveal anything meaningful about the phenomena that they purport to measure. Asked for comment about the study of super-intelligent youngsters mentioned above, geneticist Peter Visscher from the University of Queensland, Brisbane, told *Nature*: "Even for human height, where you have samples of hundreds of thousands, the prediction you'd get for a newborn person isn't very accurate." Likewise, in response to evidence about the so-called warrior gene, Harvard neuroscientist Joshua Buckholtz wrote in *NOVA* that, in his view, "any test for a single genetic marker will likely be meaningless for either explaining or predicting [individual] human behavior." And in general, the most skeptical readers of the findings from scientific studies tend to be scientists themselves.

All of which serves as a reminder that 23andMe is, in the final analysis, a marketer of data, a computer-science firm and a builder of complex correlational models. If we are convinced by what it tells us, it is only because we have implicitly accepted its premises—that our own behavior owes its origins to our biology, and that if we know everything about our genes, the events of our lives follow as night the day. Our fates are sealed on the day we are born. But these notions conflate the external markers and tools of science—the statistical methods known as "causal inference"—with scientific knowledge itself. Human understanding is broader, deeper and wider than can be contained in any formal system built *within* it. On the day when all these companies unite, bringing together all their predictive data into one über-model, will we kneel around the humming servers, in awe that we have actually built Laplace's demon? Will we then ask them how we should live our lives?

> *"Just as no one should be required to get genetic information he doesn't want, consumers should be able to find out their own genetic information when they so choose."*

The FDA Could Set Personal Genetics Rights Back Decades

Gary Marchant

In the following viewpoint, Gary Marchant argues that the recent decision by the US Food and Drug Administration, which disallows direct-to-consumer genetic tests, violates important freedom of choice about accessing private health information. Marchant claims that at-home genetic testing has many advantages and that concerns are overblown. Marchant is the Lincoln Professor of Emerging Technologies, Law, and Ethics at the Sandra Day O'Connor College of Law at Arizona State University.

As you read, consider the following questions:

1. According to Marchant, what is the problem with requiring genetic testing companies to seek premarket approval or de novo classification of its tests?

2. According to the author, does the American Medical Association support at-home genetic testing?

3. How should society deal with genetic testing companies that make fraudulent claims, according to Marchant?

The Food and Drug Administration's [FDA's] recent directive to the company 23andMe to stop marketing its genetic tests directly to consumers is a shortsighted, heavy-handed, double-standard act of paternalism. This is the last shoe to drop in the FDA's effort to wipe out the right of consumers to discover their own genetic information, some of the most important, private, useful, and interesting information about our own health and well-being. We should have a right to access that data about ourselves, but the practical impact of the FDA's action will be to put most of that data out of reach for the foreseeable future.

The FDA's Action

23andMe is the "last man standing" in the once crowded and rapidly expanding direct-to-consumer genetic test field. All the other major competitors were put out of business or stopped selling directly to consumers after the FDA sent threatening letters to all the companies in the industry a couple years ago. 23andMe tried to play ball with the FDA by starting to submit so-called 510(k) applications for some of its tests based on the tests being "substantially similar" to medical devices already on the market. Now, in the letter sent to 23andMe on Friday [November 22, 2013], the FDA indicates (correctly in my view) that the 510(k) mechanism is not appropriate, because there are no substantially similar approved tests (called "predicate devices") already on the market.

But then the FDA goes off the deep end and asserts that 23andMe must instead seek premarket approval (PMA) or de novo classification of its tests. The problem is that these regulatory approval pathways generally require clinical testing that takes several years to complete and costs millions of dollars. 23andMe or any other entrant into this field would have to pursue such approval for each test it offers—and 23andMe offers tests for more than 250 diseases and conditions. Moreover, because of rapid advances in the field of genetics, any such test would likely be outdated, replaced by a more precise and advanced test, before the clinical testing and regulatory approval could be completed for the initial test. In other words, the PMA regulatory pathway is infeasible and impracticable for these types of tests, and the FDA's insistence on such a step is a death sentence for direct-to-consumer genetic testing.

To some extent, the FDA is trapped by an outdated statutory regime that only provides the "nuclear option" of a PMA to approve DNA tests, a technology that was not envisioned when the statute was written. But the FDA was not required to take this heavy-handed and drastic action. We know this because many of the exact same genetic tests are already being provided to consumers through their physicians, without any FDA approval. There are approximately 3,000 genetic tests now commercially available through your doctor, of which only a handful have received FDA approval. So it is apparently now unlawful for 23andMe to sell *you* a genetic test but OK for your physician to order the exact same test, at a much higher cost to the consumer. This is an unjustified and unwarranted double standard.

The Advantages of At-Home Genetic Testing

There are important reasons why at-home genetic testing may be preferable to consumers. To many, their genetic information is very private, and they prefer to get the results privately at home rather than through their physician, who will likely put the information in the patient's medical record. It is much cheaper to get tested through 23andMe, which is currently of-

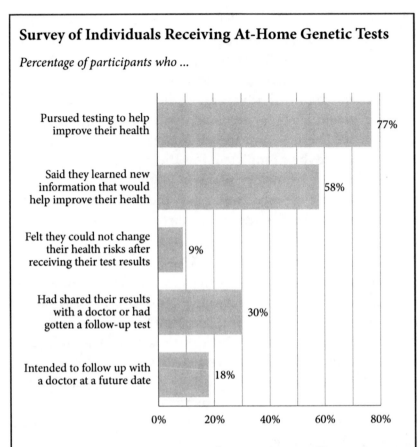

Survey of Individuals Receiving At-Home Genetic Tests

Percentage of participants who ...

Pursued testing to help improve their health — 77%

Said they learned new information that would help improve their health — 58%

Felt they could not change their health risks after receiving their test results — 9%

Had shared their results with a doctor or had gotten a follow-up test — 30%

Intended to follow up with a doctor at a future date — 18%

TAKEN FROM: American Society of Human Genetics, "Researchers Shed Light on Implications and Impact of Using Direct-to-Consumer and Clinical Genetic Testing in Disease Risk Assessment," October 20, 2010.

fering its entire battery of genetic tests for only $99. It would cost many hundreds if not thousands of dollars to get the same tests through one's physician, and health insurance does not cover the cost of most genetic tests presently. As a practical matter, most physicians are unlikely to order the complete set of genetic tests offered by 23andMe, so those who are interested and curious to get as much genetic information as possible will be blocked from doing so if they must go through their doctor.

The American Medical Association, an FDA advisory committee, and many genetics experts all support the FDA's position that genetic testing should only be permitted through your doctor. Putting aside the self-interest that may be behind some of those recommendations, it is true that a consumer who receives genetic results showing a serious health risk should discuss those results with a medical professional. But there is no need or benefit in most cases to do that up front, before a person is tested. Most physicians practicing today have little or no genetic training and simply are not in a position in the 12 minutes or so they are allotted per patient appointment to make an informed judgment or engage in in-depth discussion about what genetic testing is appropriate for a patient and what the risks and benefits are. In contrast, many consumers who seek direct-to-consumer genetic testing spend a significant amount of time learning about the genetic tests, and their pros and cons, before and after signing up for such testing. And, once they get those test results, they can and often do go to their doctor to discuss.

The FDA letter ignores all these and other advantages of at-home genetic testing and describes a parade of horribles that are greatly overstated. The FDA warns that consumers may engage in risky and perhaps unnecessary prophylactic surgery based on their genetic test results, but there are not many patients in our nation who undergo major surgery without first talking to a doctor, who will undoubtedly consider and confirm the genetic test results before operating on a patient based on those test results. The FDA expresses concern that patients will self-medicate or alter their medication doses based on their genetic test results. It is far more likely that the patient will call the genetic test results to their doctor's attention, which may provide helpful information the doctor did not have. To give a personal example, I tested positive through 23andMe for a gene variant that makes me more susceptible to bleeding from the drug warfarin, one of the examples the

FDA cited in its letter to 23andMe. My mother unfortunately recently had a mini-stroke, and the doctor in the hospital prescribed warfarin for her. She remembered that I had tested positive for the gene affecting warfarin metabolism and mentioned it to the doctor, who then decided a different drug may be better for my mother. It is quite possible that my mother did not give me that gene or that even if she did, that the normal warfarin dose would not have harmed her. But it is also possible that it would have, and my 23andMe test result brought this to the doctor's attention and allowed him to choose a different treatment option.

There are other benefits to consumers being empowered with genetic test results. Recently, 25 students in my genetics and law class at Arizona State University chose to obtain genetic testing from 23andMe. The students uniformly found the results they received useful and interesting. At least one student tested positive for a cystic fibrosis mutation, which means his children would be at a 1 in 4 risk of having this terrible disease if he happens to marry and have children with a mate also carrying the mutation, present in about 4 percent of the population. He is grateful to have this information and be in a position to avoid risking such a life-changing adverse outcome, another benefit the FDA completely ignores. Genetic information can also motivate consumers to take preventive action. Another of my students found out that she carried the ApoE4 [Apolipoprotein E4] mutation, which significantly increases the risk of late-onset Alzheimer's disease. There are no proven interventions to reduce such risks at this time, but there is suggestive evidence that exercise, mental stimulation, and perhaps certain vitamins may help reduce the risk, which she is now more motivated to undertake and which will be beneficial whether or not she is destined to develop Alzheimer's. She again is grateful to have this information and will be closely attuned to any new preventive recommendations that may be forthcoming in the upcoming decades.

The Importance of Choice

To be sure, there are real risks from direct-to-consumer genetic tests. There have been some direct-to-consumer genetic test companies that have tried to swindle consumers by selling "genetically tailored" cosmetics or "complete personality profile" genetic tests. These fly-by-night companies can be immediately detected because they do not provide the information and links to the underlying data and studies that more responsible companies like 23andMe provide. These companies offering unsubstantiated tests should be singled out for enforcement under the deceptive advertising provisions, along with the oceans of other bogus health information flooding the Internet, AM radio, and newspaper ads, rather than banning all at-home genetic testing.

Genetic test results showing major health risks can have significant psychological impacts on affected persons. For example, as the FDA notes, there can be false negatives: Home-based genetic testing does not include all the mutations for a particular health end point (e.g., breast cancer), and an at-risk person may falsely assume that he is not at any increased risk if the mutations that are tested are not present in his DNA. But this is all explained on the 23andMe website. Another of my students who also tested positive for an ApoE4 allele is less positive about learning her result than my other student and now preferred that she not know her result. But again 23andMe warns consumers about such risks, and my student does not second-guess her choice to undertake such testing— she just wishes it had come out differently. Studies are showing that consumers are generally not as psychologically devastated by adverse genetic test results as many of the experts anticipated. Arguing that consumers are too vulnerable and unable to manage such information harkens back to the bygone era of paternalism when doctors would not inform patients that they had cancer, out of fear of causing anxiety and stress. Some of these problems—which surely do not out-weigh the benefits—could be eased by better genetic education for consumers.

One thing that is absolutely clear from studies and the experience of consumer genetic testing is that people differ in their preferences about getting genetic information about themselves. Some, like me, want to get any and all the information we can. Others prefer not to know, especially for risks and traits they can do nothing about. The role of the government should be to respect and enable such choices, not to cut off that pathway altogether. Just as no one should be required to get genetic information he doesn't want, consumers should be able to find out their own genetic information when they so choose. The FDA's heavy-handed assault on 23andMe will block consumer access to our own genetic information for the foreseeable future. No company could meet the regulatory roadblocks and burdensome costs that the FDA has now imposed. This is particularly unfortunate, as we are entering an era where genetic information is increasingly relevant and useful. In such an era of opportunity and understanding, government-imposed ignorance is not bliss.

> *"It soon may be difficult to keep* any *sensitive medical problem strictly between you and your doctor."*

How ObamaCare Destroys Your Privacy

Betsy McCaughey

In the following viewpoint, Betsy McCaughey argues that the national electronic health database established by the Patient Protection and Affordable Care Act, also known as Obamacare, and the Health Information Technology for Economic and Clinical Health Act (of the 2009 stimulus package) poses privacy concerns. McCaughey claims that patients should have the right to keep certain information out of the system and should be able to control who sees the information. McCaughey is a columnist and author of Beating Obamacare: Your Handbook for the New Healthcare Law.

As you read, consider the following questions:

1. According to McCaughey, how does the 2009 stimulus legislation incentivize use of electronic health records?

2. What does the author say is wrong with proposed legislation to allow patients to request a report detailing who has viewed their information?

3. McCaughey says that in 2006 the US Supreme Court struck down an attempt by the Bush administration to do what?

Rep. Anthony Weiner announced this week that he's seeking treatment for sexual "addiction"—mortifying information that a private person would want to keep to himself. But it soon may be difficult to keep *any* sensitive medical problem strictly between you and your doctor.

The 2009 stimulus and the Obama health law enacted last year established a national electronic health database that will hold and display your lifelong medical history—making it accessible to a troubling number of strangers, including government employees and a variety of health care personnel.

Government will oversee the network linking doctors and hospitals. Doctors will have to enter your treatments in the database, and your doctors' decisions will be monitored for compliance with federal guidelines.

The stimulus legislation allocated billions for incentive payments to doctors and hospitals to become part of the network. In 2015, those incentives get replaced with penalties on the doctors and hospitals that haven't complied. And Section 1311 of the Obama health law says that private health plans can pay *only* doctors who implement whatever the federal government dictates to improve "quality." This is the first time the federal government has asserted a broad power to control how doctors treat privately insured patients.

Before the Obama health law, patients who voluntarily bought insurance shared information with their insurer. Now, government regulators will have access to oversee physician compliance.

The advantage of an electronic medical record is obvious. When you need emergency care, a doctor can get information about your past illnesses, tests and treatments with the click of a mouse. It will reduce testing, save money and sometimes save a life. But there are dangers.

Mark Rothstein, a University of Louisville School of Medicine bioethicist, worries that the system discloses information that's no longer relevant but could be embarrassing. Your oral surgeon doesn't need to know about your erectile dysfunction or your bout of depression 20 years ago. Nevertheless, such information will be visible.

Federal proposals to protect privacy have been halfhearted. On May 31, the Health and Human Services Department proposed allowing patients to request a report on who has electronically viewed their information.

After the fact is too late. Patients should have to give consent before their doctor links their record to a nationwide database, says the New York Civil Liberties Union.

The National Committee on Vital and Health Statistics, a federal advisory committee, proposed permitting patients to keep categories of information, such as mental or reproductive health, out of the national database. The Goldwater Institute, a free-market think tank suing to overturn the Obama health law, argues that the law violates privacy rights by compelling Americans to share "with millions of strangers who are not physicians confidential private and personal medical history information they do not wish to share."

Dr. David Blumenthal, appointed in 2009 to establish the national electronic medical database, explained that the goal was not "just putting machinery into offices." To reduce health consumption, doctors would have to bow to a higher authority and use "clinical decision support"—medical lingo for computers telling doctors what to do. He predicted resistance, with some doctors resigned to government penalties or demanding the law be changed.

Federal attempts to dictate how doctors treat patients will be challenged. In 2006, the US Supreme Court struck down an attempt by the Bush administration to interfere in how doctors in Oregon treat terminally ill patients. The justices would not permit "a radical shift of authority from the states to the Federal Government to define general standards of medical practice in every locality." Yet that's what the Obama health law does.

Meanwhile, the federal government is pushing ahead. Patients need to know that what occurs in their doctor's office no longer will stay there.

"*By encouraging transparency and market-based innovation around health data, we are playing to America's greatest strength to solve our most pressing problems.*"

The National Electronic Health Care Database Improves Health Care

Kathleen Sebelius

In the following viewpoint, Kathleen Sebelius argues that the rise in the use of health information technology is improving the quality of health care. Sebelius claims that there is already proof that the federal incentives to implement policies to improve care are working. She claims that the use of electronic health records has increased, and she says that the accumulation of health data is fuel for innovation in medical care. Sebelius was US secretary of health and human services from 2009 to 2014.

As you read, consider the following questions:

1. Sebelius claims that after implementing policies to incentivize better care coordination after hospital discharge, readmissions dropped by approximately how much?

Kathleen Sebelius, "Good News on Innovation and Health Care," *The White House Blog*, May 28, 2013.

2. According to the author, what fraction of hospitals are using electronic health records (EHRs)?

3. What is the purpose of the $1 billion challenge, according to the viewpoint?

A recent *New York Times* column, "Obamacare's Other Surprise," by Thomas L. Friedman, echoes what we've been hearing from health care providers and innovators: Data that support medical decision making and collaboration, dovetailing with new tools in the Affordable Care Act [also known as the Patient Protection and Affordable Care Act, or Obamacare], are spurring the innovation necessary to deliver improved health care for more people at affordable prices.

The Quality of Health Care

Today, we are focused on driving a smarter health care system focused on the quality—not quantity—of care. The health care law includes many tools to increase transparency, avoid costly mistakes and hospital readmissions, keep patients healthy, and encourage new payment and care delivery models, like Accountable Care Organizations. Health information technology is a critical underpinning to this larger strategy.

Policies like these are already driving improvements. Prior to the law, nearly one in five Medicare patients discharged from a hospital was readmitted within 30 days, at a cost of over $26 billion every year. After implementing policies to incentivize better care coordination after a hospital discharge, the 30-day, all-cause readmission rate is estimated to have dropped during 2012 to a low of 18 percent in October, after averaging 19 percent for the previous five years. This downward trend translates to about 70,000 fewer admissions in 2012.

Insurance companies are also now required to publicly justify their actions if they want to raise rates by 10% or more. Since the passage of the Affordable Care Act, the proportion of requests for double-digit rate increases fell from 75 percent in 2010 to 14 percent so far in 2013.

Reforms like these have helped slow Medicare and Medicaid spending per beneficiary to historically low rates of growth.

The Use of Health Information Technology

Last week [May 24, 2013], we reached an important milestone in the adoption of health information technology [health IT]. More than half of all doctors and other eligible providers and nearly 80 percent of hospitals are using electronic health records (EHRs) to improve care, an increase of at least 200 percent since 2008.

Friedman wrote of Dr. Jennifer Brull, a small-town Kansas family doctor, as an example of how health IT is making a difference in real patients. One of our "physician champions," Dr. Brull installed alerts in her EHRs to improve the rate of colon cancer screenings for her patients. She found colon cancer early in three patients as a result—so early that they did not need chemotherapy or radiation.

Friedman also cited several companies, like Lumeris of St. Louis, that are using health IT and "mountains" of HHS [US Department of Health and Human Services] data now in electronic form to improve health outcomes. Mike Long, the CEO [chief executive officer] of Lumeris, says his company is analyzing hospital, insurance and HHS data and getting the information to physicians in real time. "[W]e wind up delivering better care. . . . And it's lower cost," Long said.

Data as Fuel for Innovation

Since the early days of the administration, we have provided the public with high-quality health data. Making our data more accurate, available and secure brings transparency to a traditionally opaque health care market and allows innovators and entrepreneurs to use it for discovering innovative applications, products, and services to benefit the public.

Earlier this month, the administration released unprecedented data about what hospitals across the country charge for the 100 most common Medicare inpatient stays, which can vary widely. For example, average inpatient charges for hospital services in connection with a joint replacement range from $5,300 at a hospital in Ada, Okla., to $223,000 at a hospital in Monterey Park, Calif.

In May, we announced a $1 billion challenge to help jump-start innovative projects that test creative ways to deliver high-quality medical care and lower costs to people enrolled in Medicare and Medicaid.

There is much work yet to be done to change the habits of the health care system. But by encouraging transparency and market-based innovation around health data, we are playing to America's greatest strength to solve our most pressing problems.

Periodical and Internet Sources Bibliography

The following articles have been selected to supplement the diverse views presented in this chapter.

Andrea Billups — "Electronic Medical Record Expansion Raises Privacy Concerns," Newsmax, November 8, 2013.

Donna Dickenson — "Genetics for the People?," Project Syndicate, February 5, 2014.

Virginia Hughes — "It's Time to Stop Obsessing About the Dangers of Genetic Information," *Slate*, January 7, 2013.

Robert Klitzman — "Medical Privacy for Royalty and the Rest of Us," *Bioethics Forum*, December 20, 2012.

Jonathan V. Last — "Bye-Bye, Privacy," *Weekly Standard*, November 11, 2013.

Noah Levin — "A Defense of Genetic Discrimination," *Hastings Center Report*, July–August 2013.

Dinah Miller — "Medical Privacy: Gone for Good?," *Shrink Rap Today—Psychology Today* (blog), June 18, 2013.

Eric Posner — "Keep Spying on Foreigners, NSA," *Slate*, November 14, 2013.

Sean Riley and Ed Walton — "Obamacare's Privacy Nightmare," *National Review Online*, October 3, 2013.

Michael Tennant — "Say Goodbye to Medical Privacy Under ObamaCare," *New American*, June 17, 2013.

Brenda Zurita — "Patient Privacy Goes Out the Window and into the ObamaCare Data Hub," *American Thinker*, September 22, 2013.

OPPOSING
VIEWPOINTS®
SERIES

CHAPTER 4

How Should Privacy Be Protected?

Chapter Preface

There is debate both nationally and internationally about the protection of privacy. Recent advancements in technology have fueled the debate and raised challenges since the dissemination of information through technology is not completely bound by national borders. Various international agreements and national laws implement regulations for the protection of privacy. Determining how to reconcile agreements on the local, national, and international levels is one of the issues facing the future of privacy protection.

Various international agreements protect privacy, but not all countries are signatories. Article 12 of the Universal Declaration of Human Rights (UDHR), adopted by the United Nations in 1948, declared the right of privacy for individuals. It declared the right to territorial and communications privacy, referring to protection of "privacy, family, home or correspondence," as well as protection from attacks on "honour and reputation." These protections were reiterated in article 17 of the United Nations' International Covenant on Civil and Political Rights (ICCPR), adopted in 1966. Whereas the UDHR is a declaration, the ICCPR is a convention with binding commitments.

A number of signatories to the ICCPR, including the United States, made reservations to their adoption of the convention. The United States made all articles, including article 12, not subject to a private right of action within the United States, which many have argued eliminates any real enforceable rights under the convention. The enforcement of the ICCPR is challenging because of these reservations by signatory countries and because the language of the convention is open to interpretation with respect to specific situations affecting privacy.

National regulations on privacy also create controversy and confusion abroad. The European Union passed in 1995 the Data Protection Directive, which governs the protection of personal data. The European Commission is working on the General Data Protection Regulation, which will more specifically address privacy in light of new technological developments. Certain components of this draft legislation, such as the so-called right to be forgotten, are controversial. A May 2014 decision by the highest court in the European Union ruled that Google must allow users to erase links to web pages after a certain amount of time unless there are reasons for keeping them. Such a decision creates many questions concerning how Google is to implement the ruling and how it will affect the flow of information both in Europe and in the United States.

Although international agreements, regional conventions, and national and state constitutions offer protections for privacy, the extent of these protections varies. As the authors in this chapter illustrate, the United States faces many questions regarding the future regulation of privacy. Whether to extend privacy rights to foreigners and how to protect privacy on the Internet are two pressing issues that exist regarding the future protection of privacy.

"*A strong global right to electronic privacy demands recognition, in U.S. law and internationally.*"

Privacy in the Age of Surveillance

Dinah PoKempner

In the following viewpoint, Dinah PoKempner argues that the mass surveillance by the US government, its failure to extend privacy protections to foreigners, and the gradual weakening of privacy protections create an ominous example for the world and should be reversed. PoKempner claims that privacy protections have lagged behind technological change and that old doctrine applied to new situations yields poor results for privacy protection. PoKempner is general counsel for Human Rights Watch and a contributor to Foreign Policy in Focus.

As you read, consider the following questions:

1. According to PoKempner, what will happen if privacy remains strictly a domestic issue?

2. The author claims that key privacy decisions around the world have broadened the notion of privacy from "the right to be left alone" to what?

3. PoKempner claims that a big privacy loophole exists
   under section 215 of what act, and what does it allow?

President Obama had a signature opportunity in his January speech to limit the damage Edward Snowden's revelations about National Security Agency (NSA) surveillance had
done to U.S. foreign relations. But global response has been
rather cool.

Obama called for increased transparency and an institutional advocate for civil liberties before the secret court that
oversees the NSA. He recognized that foreigners have an interest in the privacy of their communications. And he announced
future restrictions on the use of acquired data as well as his
hope to move data storage out of the NSA's hands. Yet he
made clear he did not intend to end bulk collection of data or
give foreigners legal rights to defend their privacy against unwarranted U.S. spying.

A month later, European and Brazilian efforts to turn the
screws on U.S. companies over data protection continue full
steam, and foreign officials remain skeptical of U.S. intentions.
Snowden received eight Nobel Prize nominations from around
the world. On the domestic front, many also found Obama's
speech wanting ("It was a nothing burger" was legal scholar
Jonathan Turley's memorable take).

In a world where almost all aspects of daily social and
economic life have migrated online, the right to privacy has
gained in importance, and not just for the paranoid few. It is
a necessity for human rights activists and ordinary citizens
around the world to freely speak, think, and associate without
restrictions imposed by those who might wish to silence or
harm them. At the same time, corporations and governments
have acquired frightening abilities to amass and search these
endless digital records.

The United States, once at the forefront of promoting the
right to privacy as essential to modern life, has lagged behind

in legal protection even as its spying prowess has burgeoned. As a model, this is ominous, for other nations are working hard to emulate U.S. surveillance capability by bringing more and more data within their reach.

There will be no safe haven if privacy is seen as a strictly domestic issue, and legal doctrine stays stuck in pre-digital time. A strong global right to electronic privacy demands recognition, in U.S. law and internationally.

A Short History of Privacy

The United States early developed a private legal "right to be let alone." Suits against unwanted intrusion or exploitation of private details were popular, but the press fought back and often won on free expression grounds. Europe's law often put more emphasis on reputational rights.

World War II and the rise of modern surveillance states gave impetus to privacy as a defense against government abuse. The Third Reich mined census data to carry forward its genocidal policies. Many authoritarian states also deployed elaborate surveillance and data collection systems to cow their populations and suppress dissent—practices still used in places like China, Vietnam, Iran, and Ethiopia.

Privacy was invoked to limit the government's power of search and seizure. Judicially authorized warrants became a common requirement in many legal systems, and the notion of privacy of "correspondence" broadened to include new technologies, such as telephones, with laws regulating wiretaps.

The Technological Challenge

Yet protections often lagged behind technological change. In the 1928 *Olmstead* case [referring to *Olmstead v. United States*], the Supreme Court held that an unauthorized wiretap did not violate the constitutional right of the people "to be secure in their persons, houses, papers, and effects." In 1967, the court reversed course, determining that a person has "reasonable expectation of privacy" when talking in a public phone booth. This bit of common sense developed into a doctrine for when to limit government power to conduct warrantless searches.

The doctrine, however, has not always produced decisions that reflect common sense or popular expectations. Courts tend to focus more on what they think is reasonable for public safety. You may not expect warrantless aerial surveillance of your backyard, but the Supreme Court thinks that's fine, provided that what the camera sees can be observed by the naked eye. Similarly, courts have ruled that we have no expectation of privacy for information we share as business records—phone or credit card transactions, for example. Never mind that refusing to convey such information essentially bars us from engaging in many realms of modern life.

When the administration disavows indiscriminately reviewing your "private" information, it means it considers the "metadata"—the where-when-who-how long and even subject of your communications—to be "business records," no matter how detailed a portrait this provides of your daily life.

U.S. law has grown to equate privacy of communications with secrecy, an approach "ill-suited to the digital age," Justice Sonia Sotomayor said recently in a case that rejected police GPS monitoring of a vehicle for weeks on end without a warrant.

Louis Brandeis, who as a young lawyer practically invented U.S. privacy law, warned of the lag between technological leaps and doctrine. Dissenting in *Olmstead*, he wrote: "Ways may someday be developed by which the Government, without removing papers from secret drawers, can reproduce them in court, and by which it will be enabled to expose to a jury the most intimate occurrences of the home." Maybe in 1928 this sounded futuristic, but post-Snowden it seems weirdly prescient. Wiretaps eventually required warrants, but elec-

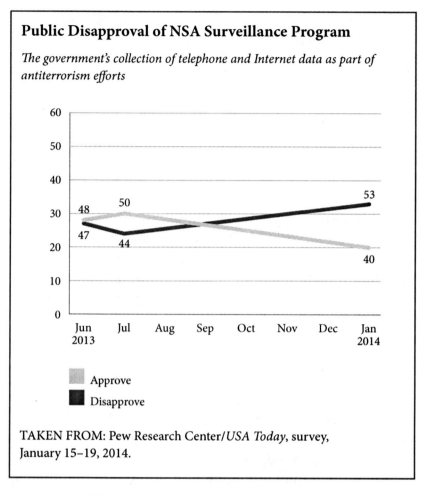

Public Disapproval of NSA Surveillance Program

The government's collection of telephone and Internet data as part of antiterrorism efforts

Approve
Disapprove

TAKEN FROM: Pew Research Center/*USA Today*, survey, January 15–19, 2014.

tronic surveillance metastasized in the 21st century under a secret regime of indulgent, minimalist judicial supervision.

A Different Path

The law in Europe took a different path. In 1983, the German constitutional court annulled the national census law, announcing "informational self-determination" as a fundamental democratic right. Integral to the modern European approach has been the belief that individuals have a right to access and correct their data held by various institutions, and ultimately to determine its use and disposal.

This approach to informational self-determination has found some parallel in a different branch of privacy jurisprudence. Key decisions around the world striking down sodomy laws and other aspects of physical autonomy have also invoked privacy, not simply as a "right to be left alone" but as a right to establish one's identity and chosen relations. This relational view of privacy is essential to protecting minorities, dissidents, and freethinkers from persecution, not to mention simply enabling the rest of us to work out who we are and what we think.

Another area where the United States led was connecting anonymity—the ultimate data protection—to freedom of speech. No doubt it helped that many of the nation's founders published revolutionary manifestos under pseudonyms. In April, the UN special rapporteur on the promotion and protection of the right to freedom of opinion, Frank LaRue, decried the "chilling effect" that restrictions on anonymity have had on the free expression of information and ideas.

The value of anonymous speech has only become more apparent in the wake of the shift of many aspects of modern life online, and the breakthroughs in our ability to store, search, collate, and analyze data with minimal cost. Anonymity now seems a last defense for both privacy and the many rights to which digital privacy provides access—such as speech, association, belief, and health.

Closing the Loopholes

Snowden's revelations of massive global surveillance inflamed an existing debate about what constitutes mass surveillance and whether it is ever justified. To understand how we got there, the loopholes knit into U.S. law are as critical to understand as the technological back doors.

The first loophole is that the United States does not consider itself bound, when its actions pose harm abroad, to respect foreigners' rights in the way the Constitution requires it to respect rights at home. Moreover, the United States tries to limit its obligations under international human rights law in the same way. Although the president may choose to selectively limit data collection for reasons of comity (calling rather than bugging Angela Merkel, for example), ordinary foreigners who pose no conceivable threat to U.S. interests can't legally challenge U.S. dragnet surveillance of their communications. Of course, the data of many U.S. citizens gets swept up in the dragnet, too.

Another big loophole is that the United States considers digital metadata to be only business records, subject to little protection. Under section 215 of the [USA] PATRIOT Act, these records can be collected if they are merely "relevant" to investigating terrorism, counterespionage, or foreign intelligence generally—and we already know the surveillance court thought virtually all U.S. call records fit that standard.

The administration has also staked a position that use, not acquisition, is the point where data privacy is at stake. But the legal view in Europe is different, and few take comfort in the notion of a foreign entity collecting their data without permission so long as no one has read it (yet). Several domestic lawsuits—including one to which Human Rights Watch is a party—are challenging this point.

Unfortunately, nothing President Obama said would really close these loopholes tightly. And nothing has yet begun to address the breach of trust caused by recent allegations that the United States systematically tried to weaken strong encryption standards, use backdoor access to technology and cable flows, or in other ways subvert the very architecture of privacy on the Internet.

Global Response

Stung by U.S. monitoring of their leaders, Germany and Brazil cosponsored a successful UN General Assembly resolution that asked the UN human rights expert to report on the harm caused by mass surveillance to privacy.

These issues will soon come before the UN Human Rights Council, the General Assembly, the European Court of Human Rights, and the U.S. Supreme Court. It would be wise for the Obama administration to modify its positions before these considerations reach the point of condemnation.

The administration can do so by immediately ending its indiscriminate, bulk interception programs, giving foreigners the same protections as citizens against unjustified invasion of privacy, ending efforts to weaken privacy protections in both the technical and legal domain, and proposing laws to help these changes survive into the next administration.

And it might help if Obama found a way to enable the man who started the debate—Edward Snowden—to come home without fearing a lifetime in prison. After all, one day they may both be Nobel laureates.

> *"As long as the world features international borders, it will be one thing for federal guns and listening apparatus to be pointing outward . . . and quite another for them to be directed inward."*

An Overreach for the NSA's Critics

Charles C.W. Cooke

In the following viewpoint, Charles C.W. Cooke argues that those who claim that foreigners abroad deserve privacy protections are mistaken. Cooke claims that the National Security Agency (NSA) is supposed to be conducting surveillance abroad to keep Americans safe and deserves no criticism for this. Whereas Cooke contends that the US Constitution protects the right to privacy of Americans and those within the country, he claims these privacy rights do not—and should not—extend beyond US borders. Cooke is a writer for National Review.

As you read, consider the following questions:

1. What piece of privacy legislation does Cooke claim is inapplicable beyond US borders?

2. According to the author, what is the root problem with surveillance by the National Security Agency (NSA)?

3. What two sets of people are entitled to the legal protection of the US Constitution, according to Cooke?

Of all the sharp instruments that have in recent years sliced open the conservative movement's belly and left it fighting for unifying stitches, the most pronounced perhaps has been the question of the National Security Agency and its regimen of surveillance. Since Edward Snowden's explosive revelations blew suddenly into the news last year, right-leaning types have sought desperately to reconcile their instinctive respect for privacy with their considered interest in security and the law. Often, they have failed to do so. At times, the fissure has even become ugly, yielding a series of set-tos between the traditionalist and libertarian wings that have inspired reports of a much-desired civil war.

Alas, those championing unity may soon find themselves reaching for the bourbon, for, having considered 46 different recommendations, the president will this week decide what shape his NSA-reform program will take, and thus in whose wounds the salt will be rubbed. Whatever he elects to do, one thing seems certain: The agency will be less powerful afterward than it was before. Among the alterations that are reportedly in the cards are requiring the FBI to obtain judicial permission before it may share the NSA's data, establishing a privacy advocate at FISA, and, most essentially, removing the federal government's power to store telephone records directly. Providing that these moves do not merely constitute distractions or sleight of hand, they will be welcome and timely— not perfect, no, but a relief for those of us who feared that the security state was destined to dig in and metastasize, thus proving the old maxim that lost liberty is never recovered.

And yet, for all the optimism inherent in the promise of change, there are small alarm bells ringing—for, making its way into a handful of news outlets is the attendant rumor that the president may decide to go one step too far, extending globally the protections of the Privacy Act of 1974 and according to foreigners bulwarks to which they have no claim. This, to put it as lightly as possible, would be a disaster.

In its story on the matter, the *Wall Street Journal* suggested that such a move would represent

> a significant shift in U.S. posture that wasn't proposed seriously until the uproar overseas in response to disclosures by Mr. Snowden, which suggested that the NSA had built a global surveillance operation that regularly scooped up communications of citizens of countries around the world, including friendly ones.

Since the affair surfaced, I have happily counted myself among the NSA's staunchest critics. But here I must break ranks with my fellow malcontents and cry foul. The reason that there had previously been no "serious" suggestion that reforming America's domestic program would necessitate changing its foreign-based regime is that such a proposal is exorbitant—the product of fluffy one-world types who haven't so much taken a libertarian exception to national-security overreach as folded the revelations into a toxic *Weltanschauung* that perceives America to be a global bully and force for ill, all alleged threats to the peace to be overblown if not deserved, and the very act of spying as contemptible. If President Obama indulges this instinct, he will be abdicating his most elemental responsibility as the chief executive of the national government: to protect Americans from those who would do them harm.

My criticisms of the NSA's conduct have been wide ranging. The sheer scale of its domestic surveillance is deeply disturbing in a country with a constitutional protection against unreasonable searches and seizures, as is the indiscriminate manner in which it has collected information. It is one thing for authorities boasting discrete permission to track individuals who are suspected of particular crimes. It is quite another for the state to turn all Americans into de facto suspects, effectively issuing unconstitutional "writs of assistance" that turn the concept of warrants on its head. Questions have abounded, too, as to whether the NSA has been operating outside of its mission and abusing the terms of its charter; as to whether the director of national intelligence, James Clapper, brazenly lied to Congress when a senator asked him about domestic surveillance; and as to whether President Obama has any real control over his own executive branch. The claim that metadata do not reveal personal information has always been risible, as has the idea that abuse and mistakes don't matter if they yield only a few victims.

The root of the problem, in other words, has been that an agency that is tasked with spying overseas has turned its attention to the homeland. It has *not* been that that agency has been doing the job with which it was tasked. The NSA isn't just *allowed* to spy broadly outside of the United States; that is precisely what it should be doing. The legal and moral questions that critics have posed to the NSA make sense only within the United States.

Proponents of the distinction that I have just established are typically accused of believing that "Americans are more important than other people," or that "only Americans have privacy rights." (It is rather unlikely that I, not being an American, would believe this.) The Declaration of Independence is thrown at us, too. After all, if all men are created equal, then why should one distinguish between victims of spying depending on their citizenship?

To the casual ear, I suspect that all of these inquiries sound rather sensible. But they do not survive sustained attention. Putting the moral questions to one side for a moment, it is indisputable that only two sets of people—American citizens and those within the country's borders—are entitled to the legal protection of the Constitution, which serves as a charter of and check on the American government and as nothing else. This isn't to say that the principles contained within the Constitution and the Declaration are not universal. Mostly, they are. But, much as I believe that my British family has a fundamental human right to free speech, they are afforded no recourse by the highest law in America. To suggest or to insinuate otherwise is, frankly, to be wrong, and I might enjoin those citing the Declaration to look a few lines down, at another part: "That to secure these rights, Governments are instituted among Men. . . ."

The moral cases are different, too. It should be self-evident that a foreign power's violating your privacy and your own government's doing so are by no means the same thing. For the vast majority of people, the practical importance of one's secrets being obtained by one's own government considerably outweigh the importance of their being obtained by a foreign power. The American federal government can and might do all sorts of immediate harm to me; the government of China, on the other hand, cannot. If a rogue official in the United States takes exception to my politics, he can make my life hell: inviting the government to track my whereabouts, ordering frivolous arrests, tying me up in endless audits and frivolous bureaucracy, and even sending a SWAT team to my house. If the Chinese politburo finds me objectionable (and I certainly hope it does), it can do very little of practical importance. Moreover, and this I think is the key point, if China tries to actually hurt me, I have distance, borders, and the American government's considerable arsenal standing in the way. If someone at home tries to hurt me, I have little individual recourse.

For as long as the world features international borders, it will be one thing for federal guns and listening apparatus to be pointing outward—protecting me from foreign foes—and quite another for them to be directed inward. The world has shrunk somewhat since the founders' time, but the validity of their belief that the domestic use of troops and force presents a threat to liberty has not. Thankfully, the internationally peculiar Anglo-American expectation that the national government may deploy troops anywhere it wishes outside of its borders but must not use them at home remains in legal force courtesy of the Posse Comitatus Act and in moral force courtesy of an ongoing American distaste for government intrusion. There is no reason that we shouldn't demand that our sleuths hew to the same principle. (While we're at it, we might also see fit to push back against the increasingly common sight of hybrid soldier-cops and military-grade SWAT teams, as documented by Radley Balko in his brilliant book *Rise of the Warrior Cop*, thus ensuring that we do not allow in a domestic standing army by another name.)

As a general rule, I suspect that those complaining about the NSA's foreign surveillance regime are as vexed by the activities that it enables as by the spying itself. Some of these activities, I also abhor. I am with Kevin D. Williamson on the question of the extrajudicial killing of American citizens, with Conor Friedersdorf in worrying about the extent of the drone war and the long-term consequences of the mistakes that are being made, and with the libertarians in feeling concerned about the scale of the security state in the post-9/11 world. Nevertheless, the problems with these activities remain the problems with these activities—not the auxiliary work that supports them. Ugly as it is to acknowledge, this is a dangerous world, and the lights of perverted science are only making it more so.

For the foreseeable future, spying will remain an indispensable part of the national defense. Reforms are necessary, yes. And I will happily man the barricades to make the case for American liberty. But behind my protest sign there will be another, declaring in no uncertain terms that this is not the time to sing "Kumbaya" and to erase from our thinking the treaty of Westphalia, and, too, that there really is no need to hobble ourselves abroad as we correct our excesses at home.

> *"There are substantially stronger reasons to worry about the collection and use of big data in the private sector than in government agencies."*

Big Data, Public and Private

Paul Pillar

In the following viewpoint, Paul Pillar argues that there exists disproportionate concern toward government collection of data than toward private company collection of data. Pillar claims that data collected by the National Security Agency (NSA) is subject to more transparency and control than data accessible by phone companies. Furthermore, he claims that the benefit from data collection by the NSA is greater than any benefit from data collection by the private sector. Pillar is a nonresident senior fellow at the Center for Security Studies at Georgetown University and a nonresident senior fellow at the Center for 21st Century Security and Intelligence at the Brookings Institution.

As you read, consider the following questions:

1. What reason does Pillar consider (and reject) as potentially the strongest basis for worrying more about government collection of data than of private collection?

2. What specific differences does Pillar identify between controls and checks on amassing data that exist for government agencies and private sector enterprises?

3. What benefit does Pillar identify with the data mining performed by the National Security Agency (NSA)?

The collection and maintaining of huge files of information on our communications, our movements, our online searching, and much else about our individual lives is, as Laura Bate notes[1], hardly something that the National Security Agency or any other arm of government originated. By far the greater share of the assembling, and the exploitation, of storehouses of data about the activities of individual Americans occurs in the private sector. So why should there be so much fuss about what a government agency may be doing along this line, while there is equanimity about the much greater amount of such activity by nongovernment enterprises? Is there something intrinsic to government that ought to make us more worried about such data mining? Let us consider the possible bases for concluding that there might be.

Potentially the strongest such basis has to do with the presence or absence of a free market, and related to that, whether or not the activity of the individuals on which data are being collected is voluntary. When I use a search engine on the Internet, I am voluntarily using a free service in return for being exposed to some advertising and allowing the operator of the search engine or my Internet service provider to collect, and exploit, data about my interests. Most interactions with government agencies and especially security agencies do not involve as much voluntarism. So maybe it is logical to be more persnickety for this reason about what government entities are doing.

That makes sense as far as it goes. But in practice, the logic quickly runs up against the fallacy of equating the private sector with free markets and free will. If I want land-line telephone service at my home (and I very much do), I'm stuck with Verizon. I am forced to let Verizon collect comprehensive records of my calls—the "metadata" we've heard so much about. And of course, if someone at Verizon wanted to listen in on the substance of my calls that could be done as well, although it is a reputable company and I would be surprised if that were happening. The point is that there is much less free will and free choice in private sector data-generating activity than we might like to think, and in many cases little or no more free choice than when a government agency is involved.

This is true not just of local utility monopolies such as land-line telephone systems but to a large degree of other services in the Internet Age. Some such services, including online access itself, have quickly transitioned from being seen as nifty innovations to being regarded as necessities. And again, free choice is often much less than we would like. This fact was recognized with the antitrust action against Microsoft, which was using its commanding position in operating systems to muscle into a bigger share of the market for browsers and other applications.

When there is enough market competition for users theoretically to vote with their feet—or with their fingers on the keyboard—if they are worried about what is being done with data collected on them, in practice any market correction mechanism would be very slow and clumsy. Imagine that a rogue employee at Google started using information about embarrassing web searches to ruin the reputations of particular people he was out to get. If that sort of abuse happened enough times, then perhaps significant numbers of users would abandon Google's wonderfully effective search engine in favor of Bing or something else, and Google would become less able to sell as much advertising as it does now. But the corrective process would be slow and awkward, and in the meantime a bunch of people would have their reputations ruined.

Another possible basis for distinguishing the amassing of data in the public and private sectors is to ask what controls or checks apply to each. Here there is indeed a big difference, and the difference is in the direction of there being far more controls and checks applied to government agencies than to private sector enterprises. For the security agencies there is the whole legal structure, dating back to the 1970s and strengthened since then, of restrictions and congressional oversight. Nothing remotely resembling those sorts of external controls exists for data mining in the private sector. Then there are all the internal checks and controls, which as Bate mentions in the case of NSA are extensive. These include compartmentation of information—second nature to the security agencies, which use compartmentation to protect sensitive national security information even if there is no issue of the personal privacy of U.S. citizens. NSA senior management says publicly[2] that only 22 people at their agency are able to query the telephone metadata that are of concern. How many people at Verizon can do something with the comprehensive record of my telephone calls? I don't have the faintest idea, and probably no one else outside Verizon does either.

Another question to ask is how the public and private sectors may differ regarding the potential for abuse, in terms of not just access and capability but also incentives. For most conceivable types of individual abuse, there is no reason to expect the incentives for individual abuse to appear more in one type of organization than the other. A potential abuser thinking of, say, looking at an ex-spouse's calling record may pop up in either the public or private sector. Disincentives to this kind of abuse probably are stronger in the security agencies, given the regular reinvestigation regimen that people with security clearances undergo.

As for incentives that are more institutional than individual, there are further differences. As an example of a mistaken and destructive use of data mining, think of an innocent person being put on a no-fly list and, as a result, having his business damaged because of his inability to fly. Government agencies have no conceivable incentive for this to happen. For them, false positives merely add clutter and make it more difficult to accomplish their assigned mission, such as keeping real terrorists off airplanes. And when a mistake of this sort does happen and becomes public, such as putting Ted Kennedy on a no-fly list, it is an embarrassment to the agencies responsible. In the private sector, however, there always are commercial and financial interests in play. Those interests may well provide an incentive—such as for competitors in the same line of business—to damage the business of someone else.

In addition to all of these criteria, one also should ask what benefit or greater good is going to the person about whom data are being collected, as well as perhaps to others. What is being bought, in other words, in return for whatever risks or intrusions are involved in amassing the data? With the sort of data mining that NSA does, the presumed benefit is in the form of greater protection against terrorists, or perhaps other contributions to national security. There has been debate, of course, about just how much of this type of benefit is being obtained, but at least the objective is one that most Americans would consider important. The corresponding answer for private sector use of big data is harder to come up with. It would seem to consist of something like better tailoring of ads that appear on the user's computer screen, which might streamline online shopping. Nice, perhaps, but hardly in the same league as national security.

Two overall conclusions follow. One is that there are substantially stronger reasons to worry about the collection and use of big data in the private sector than in government agencies.

The other is that the prevailing pattern of public consternation about this subject being nevertheless focused on government agencies indicates that the consternation is not driven by any careful consideration of risks, costs, benefits, incentives, and choices. Instead it is driven by a crude image of government agencies, and especially certain types of government agencies, as Big Brothers worthy of suspicion or even loathing. Sentiments toward private sector enterprises vary, but the biggest contrast to the image of government is enjoyed by the titans of Silicon Valley and the enterprises they run, having the status of heroes.

The crudeness driving the sentiments is one of the main reasons (inconsistency over time in what the American public expects from the government agencies involved is another big reason) we should not be surprised if morale at a place such as NSA is low.[3]

Links

1. http://nationalinterest.org/commentary/nsa-data-mining-three-points-remember-9519

2. http://www.c-spanvideo.org/program/AgencyOp

3. http://www.washingtonpost.com/world/national-security/nsa-morale-down-after-edward-snowden-revelations-former-us-officials-say/2013/12/07/24975c14-5c65-11e3-95c2-13623eb2b0e1_story.html

"The United States has a special responsibility to develop privacy practices that meet global standards and establish effective online consumer protection."

A Consumer Bill of Rights Is Needed to Protect Privacy on the Internet

White House

In the following viewpoint, the White House argues that individual privacy rights need greater protection online and Internet users need more control over their information. As such, the White House proposes a Consumer Privacy Bill of Rights that aims for individual control, transparency, respect for context, security, access and accuracy, focused collection, and accountability with respect to personal data collected online. The White House communicates the official policies of the president of the United States.

As you read, consider the following questions:

1. According to the White House, does the Consumer Privacy Bill of Rights at this point have legal force?

"Fact Sheet: Plan to Protect Privacy in the Internet Age by Adopting a Consumer Privacy Bill of Rights," www.whitehouse.gov, February 23, 2012.

2. The White House says that consumers have a right to security of data and that companies should take safeguards to protect against what sort of risks?

3. According to the author, how should companies hold employees responsible for adhering to the principles in the Consumer Privacy Bill of Rights?

The [Barack] Obama administration unveiled a "Consumer Privacy Bill of Rights" as part of a comprehensive blueprint to protect individual privacy rights and give users more control over how their information is handled. This initiative seeks to protect all Americans from having their information misused by giving users new legal and technical tools to safeguard their privacy. The blueprint will guide efforts to protect privacy and assure continued innovation in the Internet economy by providing flexible implementation mechanisms to ensure privacy rules keep up with ever-changing technologies. As a world leader in the Internet marketplace, the administration believes the United States has a special responsibility to develop privacy practices that meet global standards and establish effective online consumer protection. . . .

The Consumer Privacy Bill of Rights

The Consumer Privacy Bill of Rights applies to *personal data*, which means any data, including aggregations of data, that is linkable to a specific individual. Personal data may include data that is linked to a specific computer or other device. The administration supports federal legislation that adopts the principles of the Consumer Privacy Bill of Rights. Even without legislation, the administration will convene multistakeholder processes that use these rights as a template for codes of conduct that are enforceable by the Federal Trade Commission. These elements—the Consumer Privacy Bill of Rights, codes of conduct, and strong enforcement—will increase interoperability between the U.S. consumer data privacy framework and those of our international partners.

1. *INDIVIDUAL CONTROL: Consumers have a right to exercise control over what personal data companies collect from them and how they use it.* Companies should provide consumers appropriate control over the personal data that consumers share with others and over how companies collect, use, or disclose personal data. Companies should enable these choices by providing consumers with easily used and accessible mechanisms that reflect the scale, scope, and sensitivity of the personal data that they collect, use, or disclose, as well as the sensitivity of the uses they make of personal data. Companies should offer consumers clear and simple choices, presented at times and in ways that enable consumers to make meaningful decisions about personal data collection, use, and disclosure. Companies should offer consumers means to withdraw or limit consent that are as accessible and easily used as the methods for granting consent in the first place.

2. *TRANSPARENCY: Consumers have a right to easily understandable and accessible information about privacy and security practices.* At times and in places that are most useful to enabling consumers to gain a meaningful understanding of privacy risks and the ability to exercise individual control, companies should provide clear descriptions of what personal data they collect, why they need the data, how they will use it, when they will delete the data or de-identify it from consumers, and whether and for what purposes they may share personal data with third parties.

3. *RESPECT FOR CONTEXT: Consumers have a right to expect that companies will collect, use, and disclose personal data in ways that are consistent with the context in which consumers provide the data.* Companies should limit their use and disclosure of personal data to those purposes that are consistent with both the relationship that they have with consumers and the context in which consumers originally disclosed the

data, unless required by law to do otherwise. If companies will use or disclose personal data for other purposes, they should provide heightened transparency and individual control by disclosing these other purposes in a manner that is prominent and easily actionable by consumers at the time of data collection. If, subsequent to collection, companies decide to use or disclose personal data for purposes that are inconsistent with the context in which the data was disclosed, they must provide heightened measures of transparency and individual choice. Finally, the age and familiarity with technology of consumers who engage with a company are important elements of context. Companies should fulfill the obligations under this principle in ways that are appropriate for the age and sophistication of consumers. In particular, the principles in the Consumer Privacy Bill of Rights may require greater protections for personal data obtained from children and teenagers than for adults.

4. *SECURITY: Consumers have a right to secure and responsible handling of personal data.* Companies should assess the privacy and security risks associated with their personal data practices and maintain reasonable safeguards to control risks such as loss; unauthorized access, use, destruction, or modification; and improper disclosure.

5. *ACCESS AND ACCURACY: Consumers have a right to access and correct personal data in usable formats, in a manner that is appropriate to the sensitivity of the data and the risk of adverse consequences to consumers if the data is inaccurate.* Companies should use reasonable measures to ensure they maintain accurate personal data. Companies also should provide consumers with reasonable access to personal data that they collect or maintain about them, as well as the appropriate means and opportunity to correct inaccurate data or request its deletion or use limitation. Companies that handle personal data should construe this principle in a manner consistent with freedom of expression and freedom of the press.

In determining what measures they may use to maintain accuracy and to provide access, correction, deletion, or suppression capabilities to consumers, companies may also consider the scale, scope, and sensitivity of the personal data that they collect or maintain and the likelihood that its use may expose consumers to financial, physical, or other material harm.

6. *FOCUSED COLLECTION: Consumers have a right to reasonable limits on the personal data that companies collect and retain.* Companies should collect only as much personal data as they need to accomplish purposes specified under the Respect for Context principle. Companies should securely dispose of or de-identify personal data once they no longer need it, unless they are under a legal obligation to do otherwise.

7. *ACCOUNTABILITY: Consumers have a right to have personal data handled by companies with appropriate measures in place to assure they adhere to the Consumer Privacy Bill of Rights.* Companies should be accountable to enforcement authorities and consumers for adhering to these principles. Companies also should hold employees responsible for adhering to these principles. To achieve this end, companies should train their employees as appropriate to handle personal data consistently with these principles and regularly evaluate their performance in this regard. Where appropriate, companies should conduct full audits. Companies that disclose personal data to third parties should at a minimum ensure that the recipients are under enforceable contractual obligations to adhere to these principles, unless they are required by law to do otherwise.

> "*[Fourth Amendment doctrine] must evolve again if we are to ensure that the privacy protections the founders deemed essential to a free and vibrant democracy are not eliminated by technological default.*"

Fourth Amendment Protections Need Revision to Protect Privacy

David Cole

In the following viewpoint, David Cole argues that recent court decisions illustrate why the Fourth Amendment must evolve in order to address technological developments that now allow the government to track the movement, associations, and thoughts of its citizens. Cole contends that applying previous jurisprudence to today's technology seems to yield little privacy protection, which shows that existing law cannot effectively address modern concerns. Cole is legal affairs correspondent for the Nation *and coauthor of* Less Safe, Less Free: Why America Is Losing the War on Terror.

As you read, consider the following questions:

1. According to the author, what was the decision in the US Supreme Court case of *Smith v. Maryland*?

2. What was the majority's reasoning in the US Supreme Court case of *United States v. Jones*, according to Cole?

3. According to the author, Fourth Amendment doctrine has previously been revised to address the invention of what four technologies?

In December [2013], two federal judges reached opposite conclusions on the constitutionality of the National Security Agency's [NSA's] program for collecting and searching data on every phone call made in the United States. The first judge, Richard Leon in Washington, DC, deemed the program likely to be unconstitutional; the other, William Pauley of New York, deemed it perfectly lawful. What divided the two was the digital age itself.

Two Positions on Privacy

Judge Pauley concluded that a 1979 analog-era Supreme Court case, *Smith v. Maryland*, which allowed the government to collect the phone numbers a person has called over a short period, required him to uphold the NSA program, which collects such phone data on *every* American's *every* phone call, stores them in a massive database for five years, and uses sophisticated computers to search them for associations and networks without a warrant. Judge Leon, by contrast, concluded that the digital age fundamentally alters the kind of private information the government can glean from such records, and therefore the 1979 case does not govern. Leon is right: If we rigidly apply analog-era precedents to digital-era problems, the Fourth Amendment will no longer serve its intended purpose of protecting privacy from prying government eyes.

At first blush, Judge Pauley has a point. The Supreme Court in *Smith* reasoned that you have no expectation of privacy in the phone numbers you call because you share them with the phone company for billing purposes, and therefore the Fourth Amendment is not implicated by government collection of that information. If that is so, Pauley reasoned, why should the fact that the government is collecting those data on every American, combining them with everyone else's data and searching them, change the equation?

But it does. The government made a similar argument two years ago [in 2012] in *United States v. Jones*, which addressed whether police use of a GPS [global positioning system] to monitor a car's travel on public roads around the clock for a month implicated the Fourth Amendment. The government—relying on another analog-era precedent upholding the use of a radio transmitter beeper to help track a car from a chemical distributor to a country house—argued that no privacy concerns were raised. In *United States v. Knotts*, the Supreme Court had reasoned that the driver had no expectation of privacy, given that he was traveling on a public road from point A to point B, because anyone could watch him do so. The government argued that the GPS used to track Jones's car was just a more sophisticated beeper gathering the same public information.

But the government lost *Jones*, 9–0. The justices had different justifications, but five concluded that while we do not reasonably expect our travel from point A to point B to be private, we do have a reasonable expectation that we will not be followed 24/7 for a month, which would have been much more difficult for the police to do at the time of the Constitution's framing, and which reveals much more than a single trip.

Judge Leon similarly reasoned that although we know that the phone company will record the numbers we call, for billing purposes, we do have a reasonable expectation that it will

The Fourth Amendment

The right of the people to be secure in their persons, houses, papers, and effects, against unreasonable searches and seizures, shall not be violated, and no Warrants shall issue, but upon probable cause, supported by Oath or affirmation, and particularly describing the place to be searched, and the persons or things to be seized.

US Constitution.

not save those records for five years, collate them with those of all other phone companies and search them to identify networks of associations. As in *Jones*, the computer-aided accumulation of data can reveal a great deal more about one's private life than a single collection of data.

The Need for Fourth Amendment Revision

The broader question the NSA program raises is whether Fourth Amendment doctrine needs to be revised to account for the digital age's exponential increase in the government's ability to track us through information shared with third parties. In the old days, if the government wanted to know who all your friends were, what books you were reading and what you fantasized about, it would have to expend vast amounts of time and energy to follow you, and get a warrant to search your home—and it still would not be able to discern, for example, what you were thinking on any given day.

Today, virtually everything we do leaves a digital trace with some "third party"—our phone company, Internet service provider, e-mail server, credit card company, the bank, or the stores and online services where we shop. These companies know where we are, with whom we communicate and spend our time, what we buy and even what we're thinking. Should this mean the government can collect and analyze all these data, on the analog-era reasoning that you have no expectation of privacy regarding what you share with a third party? If so, the government could collect not just our phone records but our location data, Internet browsing patterns and purchase histories—without any individualized suspicion or court supervision. Our lives would be an open book, available to government agents whenever they chose, even if we never engaged in suspicious behavior.

If that prospect is disturbing, then Fourth Amendment doctrine has to be revised. It's been done before. It evolved to address the invention of cars, phones, thermal-imaging devices and GPS, to name just a few. It must evolve again if we are to ensure that the privacy protections the founders deemed essential to a free and vibrant democracy are not eliminated by technological default.

Periodical and Internet Sources Bibliography

The following articles have been selected to supplement the diverse views presented in this chapter.

J.M. Berger	"The Greatest Enemy of Privacy Is Ambiguity," *Foreign Policy*, October 31, 2013.
Evan Bernick	"Protecting Americans' Privacy: Why the Electronic Communications Privacy Act Should Be Amended," Heritage Foundation, February 28, 2014.
John H. Cochrane	"Think Government Is Intrusive Now? Wait Until E-Verify Kicks In," *Wall Street Journal*, August 1, 2013.
Conor Friedersdorf	"Does America Owe Foreigners Any Privacy?," *Atlantic*, January 14, 2014.
Conor Friedersdorf	"The Supreme Court Logic That Could Destroy Privacy in America," *Atlantic*, December 30, 2013.
Jim Harper	"The Internet Is Not Government's to Regulate," *Orange County Register* (Santa Ana, CA), January 19, 2012.
Orin Kerr	"Why Your Cell Phone's Location Isn't Protected by the Fourth Amendment," *New Yorker*, August 5, 2013.
Chanakya Sethi	"Do Americans Care About the Privacy of Our Metadata?," *Slate*, December 19, 2013.
Joe Wolverton II	"Fourth Amendment and Foreigners: Does It Apply?," *New American*, November 22, 2013.
Daniel Zwerdling	"Your Digital Trail: Does the Fourth Amendment Protect Us?," NPR, October 2, 2013.

For Further Discussion

Chapter 1

1. Several authors in this chapter discuss the benefits and dangers of new technologies. Drawing upon at least two authors, name the two benefits and two dangers of technology that you think are most compelling in thinking about the issue of privacy.

2. Woodrow Hartzog and Evan Selinger argue that obscurity in using technology is more important than privacy. How do they define obscurity? What are the ways in which Hartzog and Selinger say that obscurity online can be created? Do you agree that these measures can increase an individual's safety online? Why, or why not?

Chapter 2

1. Bruce Schneier argues that current state surveillance is threatening national security, whereas Gary Schmitt contends that privacy concerns are keeping security surveillance in check. Do the authors have different ideas about security that explain their apparent disagreement? Explain.

2. Tim De Chant and Katitza Rodriguez discuss the use of biometrics for identification. As fingerprints have been captured for identification purposes using ink in the past, should the digital capturing of fingerprints pose a larger concern about privacy? Why, or why not?

Chapter 3

1. Benjamin Winterhalter and Gary Marchant take opposing views on the dangers of allowing at-home genetic testing. Is it possible the concerns Winterhalter raises are not specifically about privacy? Draw upon the viewpoint of Rosa Brooks, author from the previous chapter, to develop this point.

2. Betsy McCaughey argues that the national electronic health database poses threats to privacy, while former secretary of health and human services Kathleen Sebelius argues that electronic health information improves the quality of health care. With which author do you agree more? Why? Provide specific examples to support your answer.

Chapter 4

1. Dinah PoKempner claims that privacy rights should extend globally, whereas Charles C.W. Cooke claims that the United States must only respect the privacy rights of its citizens and those within its borders. Is there a reason for thinking that any constitutional rights of Americans ought to also be granted to those abroad? If so, which rights? Defend your answer drawing upon the argument of PoKempner or Cooke.

2. Paul Pillar contends that people ought to be more worried about data collection by private companies than by the government. If he is correct, does this mean that more government regulation is needed? Why, or why not? Draw upon at least one of the other viewpoints in this chapter to defend your view.

Organizations to Contact

The editors have compiled the following list of organizations concerned with the issues debated in this book. The descriptions are derived from materials provided by the organizations. All have publications or information available for interested readers. The list was compiled on the date of publication of the present volume; the information provided here may change. Be aware that many organizations take several weeks or longer to respond to inquiries, so allow as much time as possible.

American Civil Liberties Union (ACLU)
125 Broad Street, 18th Floor, New York, NY   10004
(212) 549-2500
e-mail: infoaclu@aclu.org
website: www.aclu.org

The American Civil Liberties Union (ACLU) is a national organization that works to defend Americans' civil rights as guaranteed in the US Constitution. The ACLU works in courts, legislatures, and communities to defend First Amendment rights, the right to equal protection, the right to due process, and the right to privacy. The ACLU publishes the semiannual newsletter *Civil Liberties Alert,* as well as numerous briefings and reports, including "Surveillance Under the USA PATRIOT Act."

Brookings Institution
1775 Massachusetts Avenue NW, Washington, DC   20036
(202) 797-6000
e-mail: communications@brookings.edu
website: www.brookings.edu

The Brookings Institution is a nonprofit public policy organization that conducts independent research. The Brookings Institution uses its research to provide recommendations that advance the goals of strengthening American democracy, fostering social welfare and security, and securing a cooperative international system. It publishes a variety of books, reports, and commentary.

Cato Institute
1000 Massachusetts Avenue NW
Washington, DC   20001-5403
(202) 842-0200 • fax: (202) 842-3490
website: www.cato.org

The Cato Institute is a public policy research organization dedicated to the principles of individual liberty, limited government, free markets, and peace. The Cato Institute aims to provide clear, thoughtful, and independent analysis on vital public policy issues. It publishes numerous policy studies, two quarterly journals—*Regulation* and *Cato Journal*—and the bi-monthly *Cato Policy Report*.

Center for Security Policy
1901 Pennsylvania Avenue NW, Suite 201
Washington, DC   20006
(202) 835-9077
e-mail: info@centerforsecuritypolicy.org
website: www.centerforsecuritypolicy.org

The Center for Security Policy is a nonprofit, nonpartisan national security organization that works to establish successful national security policies through the use of diplomatic, informational, military, and economic strength. The center believes that America's national power must be preserved and properly used because it holds a unique global role in maintaining peace and stability. The center publishes periodic *Occasional Papers* and articles, all of which are available at its website.

Electronic Frontier Foundation (EFF)
815 Eddy Street, San Francisco, CA   94109
(415) 436-9333 • fax: (415) 436-9993
e-mail: info@eff.org
website: www.eff.org

The Electronic Frontier Foundation (EFF) works to promote the public interest in critical battles affecting digital rights. EFF provides legal assistance in cases where it believes it can help shape the law. EFF publishes a newsletter and reports, including "Defending Privacy at the US Border: A Guide for Travelers Carrying Digital Devices."

Electronic Privacy Information Center (EPIC)
1718 Connecticut Avenue NW, Suite 200
Washington, DC   20009
(202) 483-1140 • fax: (202) 483-1248
website: www.epic.org

The Electronic Privacy Information Center (EPIC) is a public interest research center focused on protecting privacy, the First Amendment, and constitutional values. EPIC engages in research aimed at focusing public attention on emerging civil liberties issues. EPIC publishes an online newsletter on civil liberties in the information age, the *EPIC Alert*.

Internet Education Foundation
1634 I Street NW, Suite 1100, Washington, DC   20006
(202) 638-4370 • fax: (202) 637-0968
e-mail: staff@neted.org
website: www.neted.org

The Internet Education Foundation is a nonprofit organization dedicated to educating the public and policy makers about the Internet. The foundation works to educate the public about the challenges and problems presented by the Internet. One of the foundation's projects is GetNetWise (www.getnetwise.org), an online portal with information regarding child safety, online privacy, and security issues on the Internet.

National Security Agency (NSA)
9800 Savage Road, Fort Meade, MD   20755-6248
(301) 688-6524
website: www.nsa.gov

The National Security Agency (NSA) provides information to US decision makers and military leaders. The NSA coordinates, directs, and performs activities that protect American information systems and produce foreign intelligence information. The NSA provides speeches, briefings, and reports on public information at its website.

Privacy International

62 Britton Street, London EC1M 5UY
  United Kingdom
+44 (0) 20 3422 4321
e-mail: info@privacy.org
website: www.privacyinternational.org

Privacy International's mission is to defend the right to privacy across the world and to fight surveillance and other intrusions into private life by governments and corporations. Privacy International works at national and international levels to ensure strong legal protections for privacy and seeks ways to protect privacy through the use of technology. Privacy International conducts research to raise awareness about threats to privacy and publishes reports on surveillance methods and tactics, such as "An Assessment of the EU-US Travel Surveillance Agreement."

Privacy Rights Clearinghouse

3108 Fifth Avenue, Suite A, San Diego, CA 92103
(619) 298-3396
website: www.privacyrights.org

Privacy Rights Clearinghouse is a nonprofit organization aimed at providing consumer information and consumer advocacy on issues of privacy. Privacy Rights Clearinghouse responds to privacy-related complaints from consumers and advocates for consumers' privacy rights in local, state, and federal public policy proceedings. The organization publishes and makes available on its website numerous fact sheets on consumer privacy issues.

Bibliography of Books

Lori Andrews — *I Know Who You Are and I Saw What You Did: Social Networks and the Death of Privacy.* New York: Free Press, 2013.

Julia Angwin — *Dragnet Nation: A Quest for Privacy, Security, and Freedom in a World of Relentless Surveillance.* New York: Times Books/Henry Holt, 2014.

William P. Bloss — *Under a Watchful Eye: Privacy Rights and Criminal Justice.* Santa Barbara, CA: Praeger, 2009.

Ronald J. Deibert — *Black Code: Surveillance, Privacy, and the Dark Side of the Internet.* Toronto, ON: Signal, 2013.

John C. Domino — *Civil Rights and Liberties in the 21st Century.* 3rd ed. New York: Longman, 2010.

Martin R. Dowding — *Privacy: Defending an Illusion.* Lanham, MD: Scarecrow Press, 2011.

A.C. Grayling — *Liberty in the Age of Terror: A Defence of Civil Liberties and Enlightenment Values.* New York: Bloomsbury, 2011.

Glenn Greenwald — *No Place to Hide: Edward Snowden, the NSA, and the U.S. Surveillance State.* New York: Metropolitan Book/Henry Holt, 2014.

David L. Hudson Jr. — *The Right to Privacy.* New York: Chelsea House, 2009.

Garret Keizer — *Privacy*. New York: Picador, 2012.

Frederick S. Lane — *American Privacy: The 400-Year History of Our Most Contested Right.* Boston, MA: Beacon Press, 2011.

Saul Levmore and Martha C. Nussbaum, eds. — *The Offensive Internet: Speech, Privacy, and Reputation.* Cambridge, MA: Harvard University Press, 2012.

Rebecca MacKinnon — *Consent of the Networked: The Worldwide Struggle for Internet Freedom.* New York: Basic Books, 2013.

Jon L. Mills — *Privacy: The Lost Right.* New York: Oxford University Press, 2008.

Adam D. Moore — *Privacy Rights: Moral and Legal Foundations.* University Park, PA: The Pennsylvania State University Press, 2010.

Evgeny Morozov — *The Net Delusion: The Dark Side of Internet Freedom.* New York: Public Affairs, 2012.

Cath Senker — *Privacy and Surveillance.* New York: Rosen Central, 2011.

Adriana de Souza e Silva and Jordan Frith — *Mobile Interfaces in Public Spaces: Locational Privacy, Control, and Urban Sociability.* New York: Routledge, 2012.

Robert H. Sloan and Richard Warner — *Unauthorized Access: The Crisis in Online Privacy and Security.* Boca Raton, FL: CRC Press, 2014.

Daniel J. Solove   *Nothing to Hide: The False Tradeoff Between Privacy and Security*. New Haven, CT: Yale University Press, 2011.

Cole Stryker   *Hacking the Future: Privacy, Identity, and Anonymity on the Web*. New York: Overlook Duckworth, 2012.

Patrick Tucker   *The Naked Future: What Happens in a World That Anticipates Your Every Move?* New York: Current, 2014.

Robin Tudge   *The No-Nonsense Guide to Global Surveillance*. Oxford, England: New Internationalist, 2010.

Paul Tweed   *Privacy and Libel Law: The Clash with Press Freedom*. Haywards Heath, England: Bloomsbury Professional, 2012.

Raymond Wacks   *Privacy: A Very Short Introduction*. New York: Oxford University Press, 2010.

Index

A

Abortion rights, 14
Accountable Care Organizations, 126
Acxiom Corporation, 37, 41
Afarian, Catherine, 109
Affordable Care Act. *See* Patient Protection and Affordable Care Act
Alexander, Keith, 56
Al-Qaeda terrorist network, 69
Amazon
   buying/selling data, 36
   Kindle reader, 24
   NSA comparison, 64
   success strategy, 43
American Civil Liberties Union (ACLU), 67
American Medical Association (AMA), 117
At-home genetic tests. *See* 23andMe DNA testing kit
Australia, e-passport gates, 95
Aware, Inc., 83–84

B

Balko, Radley, 146
Bartlett, Jamie, 35–42
Bate, Laura, 149, 151
Beijing Genomics Institute, 108
Big Brother Watch, 39
Bill of Rights, 14–15
Bing search engine, 150

Biometric identification technology
   development history, 83–84
   digital fingerprint recognition, 95–96
   European Union laws, 94
   facial recognition technology, 88, 94
   future potential, 19–20, 82–92
   hacking protection, 89–91
   hashing function, 89
   Homeland Security uses, 85–86
   iris (eye) scan identification, 85, 89, 97
   personal biometric uses, 88–89
   privacy concerns, 87, 93–97
   real-world uses, 91–92, 94–95
   verification needs, 84–85
Blackmun, Harry, 14
Blumenthal, David, 123
Brandeis, Louis, 136
Brazil, 134, 139
Brooks, Rosa, 65–71
Brull, Jennifer, 127
Buckholtz, Joshua, 111
Bush, George W., 109, 122, 124
Buzz (Gmail social-messaging system), 29–30

C

Carpenter, Daniel, 106
Carr, Nicholas, 21–27
Cell phones
   GPS transmitter technology, 19, 24, 37

NSA data accumulation, 36, 55–56
online data information, *25*
Centre for the Analysis of Social Media, 41
Charter of Fundamental Rights (European Union), 95
Children's Online Privacy Protection Act, 16
China, 59, 108, 135, 145
Chung, Patrick, 106
Civil liberties groups, 39–40
Cole, David, 159–163
Congress. *See* US Congress
Connecticut, Griswold v. (1965), 14, 15
Constitution. *See* US Constitution
Consumer Privacy Bill of Rights, 154–158
Contraceptive rights, 14
Cooke, Charles C. W., 141–147
Credit reports, 16, 38
Crypto-parties (online privacy workshops), 40

D

Darwin, Charles, 85
Data brokers, 37–38
Data collection
  benefits, 31–32
  consumer data companies, 38, 39–40
  ease in private information gathering, 68–69
  fears of data misinterpretation, 70
  market for drones, 79
  types of methods, 31–32
Data mining
  future potential use, 32

NSA activities, 149, 151–152
software, 23–26
user identification, 33
Data misinterpretation fears, 70
Data Protection Directive (European Union), 132
De Chant, Tim, 82–92
Declaration of Independence (US), 74, 144
Dickey, Megan Rose, 47
Digital scavengers, 36
DNA testing. *See* 23andMe DNA testing kit
Douglas, William O., 15
Drones. *See* Surveillance drones
Dunbar, Robin, 84

E

Electronic Frontier Foundation (EEF), 86, 101
Electronic health records (EHRs)
  advantages, 123
  data accuracy methods, 127–128
  hospital usage data, 126
  incentives for usage, 121–122
Electronic Privacy Information Center, 46
E-mail
  data accumulation, 36
  digital traces, 162
  Gmail, 29, 55
  NSA monitoring, 52, 87
  personal information online, *25*
  privacy violations, 29
Energy consumption pattern analysis, 41
E-passport airport gates, 95

European Court of Human Rights, 140

European Union (EU)
  airport e-passport gates, 95
  biometric data laws, 94
  Charter of Fundamental Rights, 95
  Data Protection Directive, 132
  Google legal ruling, 132

Experian, credit-reporting agency, 38

F

FAA (Federal Aviation Administration), 77–79

Facebook
  buying/selling data, 36
  creating personal details, 24
  free use trade-off, 42
  Graph Search tool, 44, 46–48
  NSA surveillance, 88
  privacy settings control, 44, 46–47
  Timeline feature, 46
  use of data brokers, 37

Facial recognition technology, 88, 94

Fair Credit Reporting Act, 16

FBI (Federal Bureau of Investigation)
  fingerprint database expansion, 86
  judicial permission requests, 142
  lies about surveillance, 58
  surveillance methods, 55–56
  use of national security letters, 61–62

Federal Aviation Administration (FAA), 77–79

Federal Trade Commission (FTC), 16, 29

Financial Services Modernization Act (1999), 16

Fingerprint identification, 85, 95–96

Fischer, Sarah, 83–84

Flu Trends Website (Google), 32, 33

Food and Drug Administration (FDA)
  halt of 23andMe DNA testing, 103, 105–106, 110, 114–115
  potential for setting back genetics rights, 113–120

Foursquare, 24

Fourth Amendment (US Constitution)
  description, 15, 162
  GPS use issue, 163
  Katz v., United States decision, 15–16
  privacy protections, needs for revision, 159–163
  protections for NSA, 61

France, use of biometric passports, 96

Franken, Al, 88–89

Friedersdorf, Conor, 146

Friedman, Thomas L., 126

G

Gait (walking) analysis, 85

Galton, Francis, 85

Gattaca (film), 107, 109

General Data Protection Regulation (European Commission), 132

Genetic Information Nondiscrimination Act (GINA), 109

Genetic testing. *See* 23andMe DNA testing kit

Germany
  knowledge/control of data, 36, 41
  NSA monitoring, 139
  World War II surveillance, 58

Global information security, 59

Gmail, 29, 55

Goldwater Institute, 123

Google
  augmented reality glasses, 40
  buying/selling data, 36
  data collection, 31, 64
  ease in private information gathering, 68–69
  European Union legal ruling, 132
  Flu Trends site, 32, 33
  FTC privacy settlement, 29
  Gmail data collection, 55
  implicit information sharing, 38
  NSA surveillance, 87
  privacy audits policy, 29–30
  rogue employee scenario, 150
  search term success, 41
  See also Schmidt, Eric

Governmental privacy concerns, 65–71

GPS (global positioning system) technology
  description, 24, 37
  Fourth Amendment issues, 163
  obscurity issues, 46
  selling of gathered information, 37
  Sotomayor, Sonia, ruling, 136
  United States v. Jones decision, 160, 161

Gramm-Leach-Bliley Act, 16

Graph Search tool (Facebook), 44, 46–48

Griswold v. Connecticut (1965), 14, 15

H

Harlan, John Marshall, II, 15–16

Hartzog, Woodrow, 43–49

Health information technology (health IT), 126, 127

Health Insurance Portability and Accountability Act (HIPAA, 1996), 100–101

Herschel, William, 85

Hill, Kashmir, 46, 47

Hines, Pierre, 76–82

HIPAA Privacy Rule, 100

Hoover, J. Edgar, 58

Human Rights Watch, 139

I

Identity theft, 40

Instagram, 39, 42

International Covenant on Civil and Political Rights (ICCPR), 131

Internet
  benefits of data sharing, 40–41
  China's surveillance use, 59
  consumer privacy bill of rights needs, 154–158
  dangers of online tracking, 21–27
  data collection benefits, 31–32
  data mining software, 23–26
  loss of anonymity, 23
  methods of buying, selling secrets, 35–42

personal defense strategy, 26–27

personal uses, 22–23

third-party tracking cookies, 36

web-browsing monitoring, 26

Iris (eye) scan identification, 85, 89, 97

J

Jain, Anil, 85, 90–91

Japan, nuclear power plant disaster, 79

Japanese-American internment camps, 64

Jefferson, Thomas, 73

Jones, United States v. (2012), 160, 161

Judeo-Christian tradition of liberty, 75

K

Katz v. United States (1967), 15–16

Kennedy, Ted, 152

Kindle reader, 24

King, Martin Luther, Jr., 58

King, Maryland v. (2013), 103, 108, 110

Klein, Ezra, 106

Knotts, United States v. (1983), 161

L

LaRue, Frank, 138

Leon, Richard, 160, 161–162

Long, Mike, 127

Lynch, Jennifer, 86, 87, 88

M

Manjoo, Farhad, 28–34

Marchant, Gary, 113–120

Maryland, Smith v. (1979), 160

Maryland v. King (2013), 103, 108, 110

McCarthy, Joseph, 58

McCaughey, Betsy, 121–124

McGregor, Matthew, 37

McNealy, Scott, 24

Medicare, 127–128

Merkel, Angela, 69, 139

Metadata collection, 57, 136, 139, 144, 150–151

Microchip technology, 40

Minority Report (film), 107, 108

Mitsubishi Electric Research Laboratories, 89–90

N

Napolitano, Andrew, 72–75

National Committee on Vital Health Statistics, 123

National Electronic Health Care Database, 125–128

National Physical Laboratory (NPL), 97

National Security Agency (NSA)
civil liberty violations, 62–64
data mining activities, 149, 151–152
debates about covert actions, 65–71
false positive errors, 153
global privacy rights violations, 52
global response to violations, 139–140
metadata collection, 150, 151

Obama, Barack, call for transparency, 134
overreach of critics, 141–147
public objection to surveillance, *137*
root problems with surveillance, 142
secrecy about capabilities, 69
security *vs.* privacy debate, 52–53
Snowden, Edward, release of documents, 52, 55–56, 66, 142–143
threat to privacy and security, no, 60–64
threat to privacy and security, yes, 54–59
transparency/control of data, 148–153
National security letters (NSLs), 61–62
Nature journal, 108, 111
New York Civil Liberties Union, 123
New Zealand, e-passport gates, 95
Nook reader, 24

O

Obama, Barack
2014, speech on intelligence, 64
call for NSA transparency, 134
Consumer Privacy Bill of Rights, 154–158
difficulty closing loopholes, 139–140
intelligence memorandum issuance, 74
responsibilities to public, 143
Obamacare. *See* Patient Protection and Affordable Care Act

Obamacare's Other Surprise (NY Times column), 126
Obscurity (concept)
defined, 44, 49
method for online creation, 44–45
public records access, 45–46
stalking risks, 47–48
Occupy Wall Street movement, 58
Office for Civil Rights (OCR), 100
Olmstead v. United States (1928), 135, 136
Open Data Institute, 41
Owad, Tom, 23–24

P

Patient Protection and Affordable Care Act
declining rate increase requests, 126–127
electronic records advantages, 123
individual privacy destruction, 121–124
Section 1311 description, 122
Paul, Rand, 67
Pauley, William, 160–161
Pew Research Center survey, 52, 53
Pickles, Nick, 39
Pillar, Paul, 148–153
PoKempner, Dinah, 133–140
Posse Comitatus Act, 146
Predator drone, 80
PRISM, surveillance program, 87, 88
Privacy Act (1974), 16, 143

R

Radio-frequency identification (RFD), 19–20, 96

Rane, Shantanu, 89–90

Reporters Committee for Freedom of the Press, US Department of Justice v. (1989), 45

Rise of the Warrior Corp (Balko), 146

Rodriguez, Katitza, 93–97

Roe v. Wade (1973), 14

Rothstein, Mark, 123

S

Satnav (satellite navigation) technology, 41

Savvides, Marios, 88, 91

Scalia, Antonin, 108

Schmidt, Eric, 26, 67

Schmitt, Gary, 60–64

Schneier, Bruce, 27, 54–59

Scientific American journal, 105

Search engines, invisibility strategy, 44–45

Sebelius, Kathleen, 125–128

Security *vs.* privacy debate, 52–53

Seife, Charles, 105

Selinger, Evan, 43–49

September 11, 2001, terrorist attacks, 56, 85–86

Shadbolt, Nigel, 41

SmartWig technology patent (Sony), 40

Smith v. Maryland (1979), 160

Snowden, Edward
  debates about leaks, 61, 138
  no imprisonment recommendation, 140
  NSA document release damage, 134
  release of NSA documents, 52, 55–56, 66, 142–143

Social media. *See* Facebook; Twitter

Solove, Daniel, 67–68

Sotomayor, Sonia, 136

Square, 91

Stalking risks, 47–48

Surveillance
  effectiveness of data collection, 56–57
  need for limitation, 58–59
  negative effects, 57–58
  NSA's privacy rights violation, 52, 133–140
  objection of public, *137*
  technological challenges, 135–137
  US governance failures, 133–140

Surveillance drones
  allowing growth of use, 76–81
  code names, 80
  consent debate, 75
  data-collection market, 79
  domestic safety concerns, 78–79
  FAA use data, 77–78
  future uses, 73–74
  legal framework needs, 80–81
  privacy issues, 79–80
  privacy threats, 72–75
  safety issues, 78–79
  use by NASA, 78

T

23andMe DNA testing kit
  advantages, 115–118

big-government concerns, 104–105
costs, 109, 116
description, 104, 109
false positives/false negatives, 103
FDA freedom of choice restriction, 103–112
genetic information concerns, 105–107
legal perspective, 103–105
need for individual choice for use, 119–120
potential uses of genetic information, 107–109
premarket approval requirement, 114–115
response debate, 110–112
survey of individuals, *116*
Third-party cookies, tracking method, 36
Tracking
benefits, 31–32
dangers of online tracking, 21–27
personal defense strategy, 26–27
personal online information, 25
privacy control dangers, 33
See also Data mining; GPS technology
Twitter, 24, 42, 67

U

UN (United Nations)
General Assembly resolution, 139
special rapporteur, 138
UN Human Rights Council, 140

UN International Covenant on Civil and Political Rights (ICCPR), 131
United Kingdom (UK)
airport e-passport gates, 95
National Policing Improvement Agency, 96
possible biometric ID use, 95–97
United States (US)
9/11/2001, terrorist attacks, 56
Bill of Rights, 14–15
closing information loopholes, 138–139
complexity of privacy, 62–64
debates about NSA's covert actions, 65–71
Declaration of Independence, 74, 144
digital fingerprint recognition uses, 95–96
drone use projections, 77
intelligence community, 61–62
Japanese-American internment camps, 64
Judeo-Christian tradition of liberty, 75
military *vs.* citizens, 73–74
national security letters, 61–62
Posse Comitatus Act, 146
United States, Katz v. (1967), 15–16
United States v. Jones (2012), 160, 161
United States v. Knotts (1983), 161
Universal Declaration of Human Rights (UDHR), 131
US Congress
Clapper, James, surveillance lie, 144
Genetic Information Nondiscrimination Act, 109

legislative gridlock, 89
oversight abilities, 57, 61
privacy legislation efforts, 33,
58, 62
US Constitution
citizens' rights to protections,
14, 74, 144–145
Fourth Amendment, 15–16,
61, 62, 159–163
home protection guarantee,
80, 138–139
Ninth Amendment, 15
types of people given legal
protection, 142, 144–145
US Department of Defense, 86
US Department of Health and
Human Services (HHS), 100,
123, 127
US Department of Homeland Security, 86, 97
US Department of Justice, 62
*US Department of Justice v. Re-
porters Committee for Freedom of
the Press* (1989), 45
US Supreme Court
Griswold v. Connecticut, 14, 15
Katz v. United States, 15–16
Maryland v. King, 103, 108,
110
Olmstead v. United States, 135,
136
Roe v. Wade, 14
role in upholding Constitu-
tion, 74
Smith v. Maryland, 160
Sotomayor, Sonia, GPS ruling,
136

terminally ill patient decision,
124
United States v. Jones, 160, 161
United States v. Knotts, 161
USA PATRIOT Act, 61–62, 139
US-VISIT (US Visitor and Immi-
grant Status Indicator
Technology), 86

V

Varian, Hal, 32
Vein matching identification, 85
Verizon, metadata collection, 150–
151
Visscher, Peter, 111
Voice analysis, 85

W

Wade, Roe v. (1973), 14
Warren, Earl, 22
Washington Post-ABC News poll
(2013), 53
Weiner, Anthony, 122
White House, 154–158
Williamson, Kevin D., 146
Winterhalter, Benjamin, 102–112
Wired Website, 46

Y

Yahoo People Search, 23

Z

Zuckerberg, Mark, 44, 46, 48

CPSIA information can be obtained
at www.ICGtesting.com
Printed in the USA
FFOW05n1517280115